Linda Kelly's books include *Juniper Hall, Richard Brinsley Sheridan* and most recently *Holland House* (I.B.Tauris). She has written for the *Washington Post*, the *New York Times*, the *Times Literary Supplement* and numerous other publications, and is a Fellow of the Royal Society of Literature and of the Wordsworth Trust. She is married to the writer Laurence Kelly, a specialist in Russian history. They have three children and live in London.

'Talleyrand's four years as French ambassador in London, his last spell as a public figure, are often overlooked in a career which had previously brought him leading roles in the French Revolution, the rule and downfall of Napoleon, and the Congress of Vienna. But his London embassy between 1830 and 1834 made an important contribution to the establishment of the July Monarchy after the Revolution of 1830, and a vital one to the creation of Belgium as a viable independent state. Linda Kelly's readable study shows how he did it, and vividly paints the leading problems and personalities with which he had to deal. She has a way of making dry diplomatic details easily understood and appreciated, and a talent for mining the sources for the most lively contemporary observations.'

WILLIAM DOYLE
Emeritus Professor of History, University of Bristol

Talleyrand and his friend Montrond playing cards, probably at
the Travellers Club, 1831. Sketch by Alfred, Comte d'Orsay.

TALLEYRAND
IN LONDON

The Master Diplomat's Last Mission

LINDA KELLY

I.B.TAURIS

LONDON · NEW YORK

To Antonia
who gave me the idea

Published in 2017 by
I.B.Tauris & Co. Ltd
London • New York
www.ibtauris.com

Copyright © 2017 Linda Kelly

ISBN: 978 1 78453 781 4
eISBN: 978 1 78672 150 1
ePDF: 978 1 78673 150 0

A full CIP record for this book is available from the British Library

A full CIP record is available from the Library of Congress

Library of Congress Catalog Card Number: available

Typeset by Tetragon, London
Printed and bound in Sweden by ScandBook AB

MIX
Paper from
responsible sources
FSC® C007584

Contents

	List of Illustrations	ix
	Supporting Cast	xi
	Author's Note	xv
	Prologue	1
1 ·	The July Revolution	9
2 ·	Ambassador in London	18
3 ·	The Belgian Conference	27
4 ·	Social Successes	37
5 ·	The Search for a Monarch	45
6 ·	The Eighteen Articles	53
7 ·	French Troops in Belgium!	63
8 ·	'A Firm and Cordial *Entente*'	74
9 ·	The Triumph of Reform	82
10 ·	Leave of Absence	92
11 ·	Besieging Antwerp	101
12 ·	A New Challenge	110
13 ·	The Quadruple Alliance	118
14 ·	A Changing Scene	127
15 ·	Time to Go	137
	Epilogue	149
	Notes	153
	Bibliography	161
	Index	163

List of Illustrations

FRONTISPIECE: *Le prince de Talleyrand & Mr Montrond jouant au whist fait par le comte Alfred d'Orsay.* (Richard von Hünersdorff, 1831.)

1. Charles-Maurice, Prince de Talleyrand Périgord. (After Ary Scheffer, 1828. National Portrait Gallery.)

2. The Duchesse de Dino, from the frontispiece to her memoirs, 1831–62.

3. The Duc d'Orléans takes the oath as Louis-Philippe I, king of the French, in the Chamber of Deputies on 9 August 1830. (Lithograph by Lemercier.)

4. The July Revolution: battle at the rue de Rohan, 29 July 1830, by Hippolyte Lecomte. (Bridgeman Library.)

5. Adélaïde d'Orléans by Marie-Amélie Cogniet, 1838. (Bridgeman Library.)

6. *The Protocol Society in an Uproar, or the Conferees Confounded.* Etching by S. W. Fores after Henry Heath, *c.* August 1831. (Richard von Hünersdorff.)

7. *The Library at Holland House* by C. R.Leslie, 1838. (Private collection.)

8. *A Tête à Tête*, Lord Holland and Talleyrand. Cartoon by HB [John Doyle], 1831.

9. Lord Palmerston by Conrad L'Allemand, *c.*1830s–40s.

10. *The Lame Leading the Blind*, Talleyrand and Lord Palmerston. Cartoon by HB [John Doyle], January 1832. (National Portrait Gallery.)

11. William IV by James Lonsdale, 1830. (National Portrait Gallery.)

12. Leopold I, king of the Belgians, after George Dawe, *c.*1830s–40s. (National Portrait Gallery.)

13. Princess Lieven from a drawing by John Lucas, *c.*1830s.

14. *La Quadruple Alliance.* Illustration to *La caricature*, No. 200, September 1834. (Richard von Hünersdorff.)

15. *L'apoplexie allant remplacer à Londres la paralysie* by Honoré Daumier for *La caricature*, No. 225, 26 February 1835. (Richard von Hünersdorff.)

16. Valençay, a nineteenth-century view of Talleyrand's chateau in Berry, bought at the suggestion of Napoleon in 1803. (Éléonore Berry.)

COVER: The image of Talleyrand is taken from his portrait by Carl Vogel, drawn during a visit to London on 26 June, 1834, reproduced in lithograph facsimile by Ludwig Zöllner. (Richard von Hünersdorff.)

Supporting Cast

Aberdeen, George Gordon, Earl of (1784–1860)

Foreign secretary under Wellington 1828–November 1830, and prime minister 1852–5.

Bacourt, Louis Adolphe, Comte de (1801–65)

Principal secretary at the French embassy in London 1831–5.

Berry, Maria Carolina, Duchesse de (1793–1870)

Mother of Charles X's grandson, the Duc de Bordeaux, the legitimate heir to the French throne after Charles's abdication.

Broglie, Victor Francois, third Duc de (1785–1870)

French minister of foreign affairs October 1832–March 1833.

Bülow, Heinrich, Baron von (1792–1846)

Prussian ambassador in London 1827–41.

Charles X (1757–1845)

King of France 1824–30. Forced to abdicate following the July Revolution of 1830, he was succeeded as king of the French by his cousin Louis-Philippe I.

Dino, Dorothea, Duchesse de (1793–1862)

Daughter of the Duke of Courland; married to Talleyrand's nephew, Edmond de Talleyrand-Périgord, Duc de Dino. Separated from her husband after the birth of her three children, she became the companion, and possibly mistress, of Talleyrand, acting as his hostess at the Congress of Vienna and the French embassy in London.

Esterházy, Prince Paul (1786–1866)

Austrian ambassador in London 1816–19 and 1830–9. Married to a niece of the empress of Austria, he was said to be one of the richest men in Europe.

Flahaut, Charles de Flahaut de La Billarderie, Comte de (1785–1870)

Talleyrand's son by his mistress the Comtesse de Flahaut. Exiled to Britain after Waterloo, where he served as Napoleon's aide-de-camp, he married a Scottish heiress, Margaret Mercer Elphinstone, Viscountess Keith.

Granville, Granville Leveson-Gower, first Earl (1773–1846)

British ambassador in Paris 1824–8 and 1830–41. His wife Harriet, a sister of the Duke of Devonshire, was a leading figure in Paris and London society.

Grey, Charles, second Earl (1754–1845)

Leader of the Whig opposition from 1806 and prime minister 1830–4, he was responsible for steering the Reform Bill of 1832 through Parliament.

Holland, Elizabeth, Lady (1771–1845)

Divorced from her first husband, Sir Godfrey Webster, she was ostracised in many London drawing rooms, but created her own salon at Holland House in Kensington – a celebrated centre of political and intellectual life.

Holland, Henry Vassall-Fox, third Baron (1773–1840)

Nephew of Charles James Fox and an old friend of Talleyrand's, he used the influence of Holland House and his position in Grey's Cabinet to further Anglo-French relations during the negotiations over Belgium.

Leopold I (1791–1865)

Married to the Prince Regent's daughter, Princess Charlotte, in 1816, and widowed the following year, Leopold of Saxe-Coburg came to the throne as king of the Belgians in 1831. His marriage to a daughter of Louis-Philippe helped calm French fears that he was too pro-British.

Lieven, Count (later Prince) Christopher von (1774–1839)

Russian ambassador in London 1812–34. An able but colourless diplomat, he was overshadowed by his charismatic wife Dorothea, Princess Lieven, the leading diplomatic hostess of her time.

Louis-Philippe I (1772–1850)

Son of Philippe Égalité, who signed the death warrant of Louis XVI and a general in the revolutionary army at Jemappes, he came to the throne as king of the French – 'the citizen king' – following the revolution of July 1830. His wife, Marie-Amélie, daughter of Ferdinand IV of Naples and Sicily, was a niece of Marie Antoinette.

Molé, Louis-Mathieu, Comte (1781–1855)

Minister of foreign affairs in Louis-Philippe's first Cabinet, August to November 1830, and prime minister 1836–9.

Montrond, Casimir, Comte de (1765–1843)

One of Talleyrand's oldest friends and his confidential agent in many of his financial dealings.

Orléans, Adélaïde, Princesse d' (1777–1847)

Younger sister of Louis-Philippe I. Devoted to her brother, whom she helped to seize the throne, she was his closest personal adviser on political matters, especially on foreign affairs.

Palmerston, Henry John Temple, third Viscount (1764–1865)

He began his political life as a Tory, but switched to the Whigs in 1830, serving as foreign secretary under every Whig administration between 1830 and 1851. He was prime minister 1855–8 and 1859–65.

Périer, Casimir (1777–1832)

French prime minister November 1830–May 1832. Largely successful in bringing stability and order to France after the troubled first months of Louis-Philippe's reign. His premature death, after a visit to the victims of cholera during the Paris epidemic of 1832, was a major blow to the regime.

Rigny, Henri, Comte de (1782–1835)

A former admiral, and minister for the navy under Louis-Philippe, he was minister for foreign affairs 1834–5. He worked closely with Talleyrand over the Quadruple Alliance.

Sébastiani [de La Porta], Horace François Bastien, Comte (1772–1851)

A Napoleonic general and former ambassador to Turkey, Sébastiani was minister of foreign affairs November 1830–January 1831. He succeeded Talleyrand as French ambassador in London in 1835.

Van de Weyer, Sylvain (1802–72)

Belgium's first representative in London, following the Belgian revolution of 1830. He would later become prime minister of Belgium.

Vaudémont, Louise de Montmorency, Princesse de (1763–1832)

An old friend of Talleyrand, and an intimate of Louis-Philippe and his sister, she acted as Talleyrand's unofficial intermediary during his embassy in London.

William I (1771–1843)

Prince of Orange-Nassau; king of the United Kingdom of the Netherlands 1815–30, he was left as king of Holland and Grand Duke of Luxembourg after the establishment of Belgium as an independent state.

William IV (1765–1837)

The third son of George III, he inherited the throne of the United Kingdom of Great Britain and Ireland from his brother George IV in 1830. He was married to Adelaide of Saxe-Meiningen.

Author's Note

WHETHER hated or loved by his contemporaries, Charles-Maurice, Prince de Talleyrand-Périgord was generally regarded as the master diplomatist of his age. Famously enigmatic, he played his cards close to his chest – 'I wonder what he meant,' Metternich is said to have asked when he heard that Talleyrand had died.

There have been many outstanding biographies of Talleyrand, from Duff Cooper's 1930s classic (which has never been out of print) to the most recent life in French, *Talleyrand: le prince immobile* by Emmanuel de Waresquiel. But Talleyrand's career was so crowded and so linked with the turbulent events of his time that there have been many books too which deal with just a single aspect of his life. I think in particular of Michel Poniatowski's sparkling biographical studies, *Talleyrand aux États-Unis*, *Talleyrand et le consulat* and others, each of which deals – in much more detail than would be possible in a full-length biography – with a decisive period in his career. As far as I know, however, there has been no such close-up coverage of Talleyrand's four years as ambassador in London, the last great mission of his diplomatic life and in his own opinion the most important. 'I have done a little good,' he said later; 'it is my best work.'[1] It is these four years which are the subject of this book.

Talleyrand's character was shaped by the dramatic happenings through which he lived. It would be hard to find a better summing up of his career before coming to London than that of the diarist and politician Charles Greville, a frequent visitor to the French embassy while Talleyrand was in residence:

Born at the end of the reign of Louis XV, and bred up in the social pleasures and corruptions of that polite but vicious aristocracy, he was distinguished in his early youth for his successful gallantries... A debauched abbé and bishop, one of the champions and then the victims of the Revolution (having scrambled through the period of Terrorism), discarding his clerical character, he became Minister of the Consulate and the Empire, and was looked upon all over Europe as a man of consummate ability, but totally destitute of principle in public or in private life. Disgraced by Napoleon, he reappeared after his fall and was greatly concerned in the restoration of the Bourbons. For a short time only he was employed by them, but always treated by them with respect and consideration. The Revolution of July again brought Talleyrand prominently on the stage and, to the surprise of all men, he accepted the embassy in London.[2]

Talleyrand was 76 when he came to London, an age which, by the standards of his time, not many people even reached. He looked every day of his age. Wellington's friend Mrs Arbuthnot, who had known him in Paris in 1815, when she thought him 'the most agreeable man she knew', found him just as agreeable but even uglier in 1830: 'Really hardly human, as old as Methusalem, with a most enormous quantity of powdered hair.'[3] But the success of his mission was amazing. At a time when the affairs of Britain were almost exclusively the preserve of the aristocracy, politics was intimately connected with the social life of London. Talleyrand's princely status, the charm of his conversation and the grandeur with which he entertained were an essential part of his diplomacy. Supported by his niece and hostess, the Duchesse de Dino, 39 years younger than him and reputedly his mistress, he made the French embassy one of the most brilliant and fashionable places in London.

Arriving in the wake of the July Revolution, with Louis-Philippe still barely established on the throne, Talleyrand knew that good relations between his country and Britain, a constitutional monarchy like France's own, were vital to ensuring its acceptance by the other European powers. He also knew that war would be fatal to the new regime. In this he was at one with Louis-Philippe, whose rise to power he had helped to mastermind. The partnership between them would be one of the main factors in keeping the peace in the early 1830s, when revolutions were breaking out across Europe and France was viewed with deep suspicion by the autocratic powers. To all intents and purposes he was Louis-Philippe's foreign minister during the first years of his reign.

Talleyrand's memoirs, based largely on contemporary letters and despatches, are the chief source for the diplomatic history of his time in London. They are supplemented on a personal level by the journals of the Duchesse de Dino; by Talleyrand's letters (still unpublished) to his great friend Lord Holland, whose salon at Holland House was the unofficial headquarters of the Whig party, and by the journals of Holland himself. But almost everyone who was anyone in London, from diarists to journalists and politicians, had something to say about Talleyrand, and their impressions fill out the picture of his embassy as seen through British eyes. Of special interest are the ups and downs of his relations with Palmerston, the foreign secretary, nearly 30 years his junior and determined not to be bamboozled by the older man. Was it for this reason that he always referred to Talleyrand as 'old Talley', as if to cut him down to size? Between them, however, they achieved the near impossible. The July Revolution in France had inspired a knock-on revolution by the Belgians, determined to break away from Holland, to which they had been united after 1815. The peaceful establishment of Belgium as an independent and neutral country, in the teeth of the autocratic states of Russia, Austria and Prussia, was the joint work of Palmerston and Talleyrand. The neutrality of Belgium remained unchallenged till the Germans invaded it in 1914, and the outlines of Europe were changed forever.

Two points in the text need explaining. The first is that in the diplomatic exchanges of the nineteenth century Britain is usually referred to as England. I have left the word England as given when quoting from contemporary documents but have otherwise referred to Britain. The second is to do with Foreign Office usage. All the letters from the British Foreign Office to Talleyrand were in French, the official diplomatic language of the day. It was not until 1834 that Palmerston made the rule, which has been followed ever since, that diplomatic letters should be written in English in order to be readily understood by Parliament. The English versions of Palmerston's and other Foreign Office letters quoted here – in common with other translations in this book – are therefore my own.

Talleyrand is still an honoured presence at the French embassy in London, where his magnificent portrait by Gérard, painted in 1808, hangs on the staircase of the ambassador's residence in Kensington Palace Gardens; lofty and inscrutable, he is shown in court dress, the rich blue velvet of his coat reflected in his eyes. I am told that his maxim 'diplomacy begins with the cuisine' is still quoted when receptions are in preparation. I am very grateful to Rosie Gorman, *chef de protocole* at the French embassy, for arranging for me to see this painting.

I am very grateful, too, to the staff of the Kensington Central Library, the London Library and the Manuscripts Room of the British Library; to Richard von Hünersdorff for permission to reproduce images from his remarkable collection of books, prints, drawings, autographs and manuscripts in relation to Talleyrand, and to Robin Halwas for introducing me to the collection in the first place; to Professor Munro Price and Comte Thierry de Sayve for generously sparing the time to read my book in manuscript; to Dr Philip Mansel for sending me the text of his lecture on the creation of Belgium which I first heard at the Belgian embassy; to Éléonore Berry, direct descendant of the Duchesse de Dino, for allowing me to reproduce her print of the Château de Valencay; to Guy Penman for his help in tracking down cartoons of Talleyrand; to Nicholas Baring for permission to consult the Talleyrand letters in the Baring archive; to Lucie Campos Mitchell, head of the book office and Louise Cambau, book officer at the Institut Français; to Sheila Markham, librarian of the Travellers Club; to my agent and former publisher Christopher Sinclair-Stevenson; to my editors, Dr Lester Crook, Sophie Campbell and Joanna Godfrey at I.B.Tauris and Alex Billington and Alex Middleton at Tetragon Publishing; to friends and relations for their help and encouragement: John Boyd, Antonia Fraser, Virginia Fraser, Rosanna Gardner, Rachel Grigg, Eliza Hoyer Millar, Nicholas Kelly, Chip Martin, Douglas Matthews, Mollie and John Julius Norwich, Jeremy O'Sullivan, Valerie Pakenham, the late Kenneth Rose, Francis Russell, Anne Thorold, Marie-Laure de Varennes de Buel, Humphry and Katherine Wakefield, Frances Wilson and Philip Ziegler; and last but certainly not least to my husband Laurence Kelly for his constant interest and support.

Prologue

Paris, 31 August 1792. Eleven o'clock in the evening. In an anteroom of the Palais de Justice, Charles-Maurice de Talleyrand-Périgord, the former bishop of Autun, is waiting to see Danton, the minister of justice. He is dressed for travel: booted, with a long coat, a round hat, and his hair tied back in a queue. The scene is described in the memoirs of the Jacobin deputy Bertrand Barère, a former colleague of Talleyrand's in the Constituent Assembly. 'I had known him well for three years in the assembly,' he wrote.

> He came up to me in a friendly way; he could see that I was astonished at finding him at the Ministry of Justice so late at night. 'It's because I'm expecting to leave for London on a government mission in the morning,' he told me. 'I've come to collect the passport which Danton should be bringing me after the meeting of the executive council which is going on at this minute.'[1]

Talleyrand waited for Danton till 1.30 in the morning, but when the minister arrived he was empty-handed. The executive council, he explained, had been too busy to discuss his passport. Since April France had been at war, its eastern frontiers threatened by the armies of Austria and Prussia. Six days earlier the border fortress of Longwy had fallen to the enemy; the nearby fortress of Verdun was now under siege and unlikely to hold out for long. In the midst of this national crisis it was hardly surprising that Talleyrand's papers had been overlooked.

Ever since 10 August, when the mob had stormed the palace of the Tuileries, massacring the Swiss Guard and forcing the king and the royal family to take refuge in the Legislative Assembly, Talleyrand's life had been in danger. Like most of his friends, he belonged to that group of liberal or moderate politicians who had welcomed the opening stages of the Revolution as a chance to combine reform with a constitutional monarchy. The tenth of August had seen the ruin of their hopes. The king and his family were now prisoners in the Temple; an insurrection-ary government, with Danton among its leaders, had taken over. Those of Talleyrand's fellow constitutionalists who had not already fled were either in prison or on the run. His own position was only slightly more secure. Having spent the early summer on a mission to London to ensure Britain's neutrality in the war, he had bought time – and the promise of a passport – by drafting a letter to the British and other foreign gov-ernments justifying the king's suspension on the grounds that he had tried to undermine the constitution. It was not a document of which he could be proud but he had done his best to save the monarchy while he could; he was now fighting for survival. Many of his friends had already escaped to England. Talleyrand was desperate to follow them, but he was determined to do so officially. 'I wished to leave the country with a regular passport,' he wrote later, 'so that I would not be barred forever from returning there.'[2] It was this passport which he had been awaiting in the early hours of 1 September.

At ten o'clock on the morning of 2 September came the news that the fortress of Verdun had fallen. The way to Paris was now wide open for the invading armies. Church bells sounded the alarm; armed crowds gath-ered in the streets and Danton, in the Legislative Assembly, exhorted his fellow deputies to 'dare and dare and dare again'. At four in the afternoon, on the pretext that the prisoners were counter-revolutionaries, plotting to join forces with the enemy, the massacres in the prisons began. Over the next five days more than a thousand prisoners were murdered by the mob, the killing spreading to the streets, where so-called enemies of the people were dragged from their houses and massacred in their turn. Day after day Talleyrand called at Danton's office, not knowing whether the next would be his last. Finally, on the evening of 8 September, he was rewarded with his passport, duly signed and counter-signed, allowing him to leave for London. 'Danton saved my life,' he declared later.

The September massacres, in Danton's defiant words, put 'a river of blood' between Paris and the invading armies. On 20 September, the enemy advance was checked at the Battle of Valmy, the first great victory of the revolutionary army; by mid-October Longwy and Verdun had been recaptured, and the allied troops had been forced back across the frontier. But the horror of the massacres had stained the glory of France's victories, filling even those who had been most sympathetic to the Revolution's aims with revulsion.

For Talleyrand and his fellow constitutionalists it was a moment of utter disillusion. Only three years earlier, with the meeting of the States General in 1789, the century approaching its last decade – the famous century of enlightenment and reason – had seemed to be reaching its zenith. In every branch of France's intellectual life new ideas had changed the expectations of the age, undermining its institutions without as yet destroying them. Still possessing the privileges of the past but filled with generous aspirations for the future, the liberal aristocracy stood poised between two eras. It was an enchanted if delusory pause. 'If I by sacrificing the memory of that brief period of light and glory,' wrote Talleyrand years later, 'could add ten years to my life *now* I would not do it.'[3]

The bright dream had turned into a nightmare, leaving the constitutionalists to face the execration of both the new and old regimes. Having escaped death at the hands of the revolutionaries, they were greeted in London by the hatred of the ultra-royalist émigrés who had fled to England two years earlier and who held their policies responsible for the downfall of the monarchy. Their hatred was nothing new to Talleyrand. He had experienced the malice of the émigrés on his visit to London earlier that year, when they had done everything to embarrass and impede his mission. He had fared little better with English society: he had been snubbed by the foreign minister, cold-shouldered by the court and dismissed by the arch-gossip Horace Walpole as a 'viper who has cast his skin'.[4] (Talleyrand, lame since childhood, had been forced by his family to join the Church; having led the move to confiscate the Church's property in 1789, he was excommunicated two years later.) Only the leaders of the Whig opposition, liberal aristocrats sympathetic to the Revolution's original aims, were still prepared to welcome him: they included the great Whig statesman Charles James Fox and the former prime minister the Marquess of Lansdowne, whose magnificent house at Bowood in Wiltshire was a centre of scientific and intellectual life. 'When one has lived through two months like the last,' wrote Talleyrand gratefully to Lansdowne,

> one has a real need for the company of enlightened minds. At a time when everything has been perverted and distorted, those who remain faithful to the ideal of Liberty, despite the atrocious mask of filth and blood with which it has been obscured by scoundrels, are all too few in number.[5]

With Lansdowne, Fox and other leading members of the Whig opposition, Talleyrand not only had the sympathy of those who shared his progressive views but a chance to see how a representative monarchy along the lines envisaged by the constitutionalists worked out in practice. The Whig opposition, outspoken in its defence of civil liberties, was an important part of the system. Amid fears that the revolutionary contagion would spread to Britain, the Tory government was growing increasingly repressive; it was thanks to the efforts of the Whigs, above all Fox, in Parliament that the rights of free speech and free assembly were never totally extinguished.

Gradually, as September went by the friends and allies from the constitutionalist party who had managed to escape from France made their way to London. So too did the women who had formed part of their circle, among them Talleyrand's mistress, the Comtesse de Flahaut, and their small son; her much older husband (the official father of her child), who remained behind, would die on the scaffold the following year. Most of the new arrivals were penniless or very nearly so; Talleyrand himself would be forced to sell his precious library, which he had shipped to London earlier, to survive. But even in adversity they continued to enjoy the pleasures of good company and conversation. For the brilliant and witty society of pre-revolutionary Paris conversation had almost been the reason for existence; to be deprived of it in London would have been a fate still worse than poverty. In garrets and threadbare lodgings they kept up the graces of their Paris drawing rooms, and the wit and sparkle of the company made up for the sparseness of the fare. 'I promise not to look surprised,' whispered Talleyrand to his old friend, the Comtesse de Genlis, when thanks to an unexpected windfall she managed to give her guests a decent meal.[6]

Meanwhile, events across the Channel were plunging ever deeper into anarchy and bloodshed. France had been declared a republic; the fate of the king and royal family aroused the direst expectations. Talleyrand had remained informally in touch with the revolutionary government during his first weeks in London. But his semi-official position changed dramatically when on 15 November a safe containing secret papers was discovered in the king's apartments in the Tuileries. Among the letters found there were two in which Talleyrand was mentioned as someone who was ready to offer his services to the king. It did not matter that the letters were written in March, when the king was still the head of state; they were enough to brand Talleyrand as a traitor in the revolutionary government's eyes. His property in France, together with that of most of his family, was confiscated; his name was entered on the list of proscribed – or wanted – émigrés, and his description circulated to the authorities: 'Height: five foot three inches tall [in fact he was considerably taller]... blue eyes, nose slightly retroussé... limps on one foot, either the left or right.'[7]

Talleyrand had protested to the National Convention at being judged without a hearing, but in reality his condemnation came as a relief. He could no longer be associated with the French government or its actions, a fact of supreme importance when, on 21 January 1793, to the horror of all Europe, and the anguish of the constitutionalists, who felt that their policies had been in part responsible, Louis XVI was executed. Ten days later France declared war on Britain.

With the outbreak of the war, the position of the constitutionalists became more difficult than ever. While Talleyrand stayed in London, to keep his ear to the ground, a number of his friends sought seclusion in the countryside, away from the hostility of the royalist émigrés and the suspicions of the authorities. One such group included the former minister of war, the Comte de Narbonne, the lover of Talleyrand's old friend (and former mistress) Madame de Staël, who rented a house near Dorking called Juniper Hall, where their illustrious titles, progressive politics and unconventional morals alarmed and fascinated their Surrey neighbours.

Madame de Staël's arrival from Switzerland to join Narbonne in January 1793 brought Talleyrand hurrying down to Surrey to see her, perhaps to try his luck again – she was always generous with her favours – but in any case to enjoy the brilliance of her company and the atmosphere of intellectual excitement she diffused around her. Madame de Flahaut, meanwhile, was having an affair with Lord Lansdowne's son, Lord Wycombe – which did not prevent her from staying on friendly terms with Talleyrand. 'There was absolute disorder in such matters,' he wrote later.[8]

Staying near Juniper Hall with her sister Susanna Phillips was the novelist Fanny Burney; deeply sympathetic to their plight, she and her sister soon became friends with the French exiles and she describes them vividly in her letters home. Fanny Burney was no stranger to good conversation. She had been the darling of Dr Johnson; she moved in a society which included Sheridan, Burke and Garrick. But she was completely bowled over by the charm of her new neighbours. Of Talleyrand at first she was a little doubtful:

'How do you like him?' whispered Madame de Staël.

'Not very much,' replied Fanny, 'but then I do not know him.'

'Oh, I assure you,' cried Madame de Staël, '*he is the best of the men.*'

Before long Fanny Burney was forced to agree. 'It is inconceivable what a convert M. de Talleyrand has made of me,' she wrote to her father. 'I think him now one of the first members & one of the most charming of this exquisite set... His powers of entertainment are astonishing, both in information & in raillery.'[9]

Fanny was charmed but the outside world did not share her admiration. Talleyrand's revolutionary past, his rejection of the Church and his relationship with Madame de Staël, herself a hated figure to the émigrés, were enough to damn him in most people's eyes. Throughout the dreadful year of 1793, as the Terror gathered pace, he deliberately kept a low profile. Looking back on that period later, he found it impossible to recall the sequence of events. The notes he had written at the time were meaningless. 'Their thread is lost to me... I tried too often to avert my eyes from those hideous events, where so much ferocity was mixed with so much degradation, to be able to describe them.'[10] Powerless to act or to influence what was happening, he passed his time, according to his memoirs, in fishing and correcting proofs for Madame de Flahaut. Her novel *Adèle de Sénange*, based on her own experiences and the moral dilemmas – which had not bothered her too greatly – of a young woman married to a much older man, was a best-seller when it appeared the following year.

By this time, however, Talleyrand had left England. To the authorities he had always been a 'deep and dangerous man', not only a friend of left-wing figures such as Fox but the best-known and most hated of the constitutionalists. The war with France was going badly; the execution of Marie Antoinette in October had increased the revulsion with which the revolutionary government was regarded. Fear and suspicion of the

French in Britain were reaching hysterical proportions; the Alien Bill, making it possible for foreigners to be expelled without notice, made their position still more insecure. In this atmosphere of wartime paranoia Talleyrand was a natural target for the bill.

In February 1794 the blow fell. 'Last Tuesday, at five o'clock in the evening,' wrote Talleyrand to Madame de Staël, 'two men appeared at my door, one of whom told me he was a messenger of the state and that he had come to serve an order from the king that I must leave his kingdom within five days.'[11]

Madame de Staël had returned to Switzerland the previous summer, where her home had become a haven for friends escaping from France. But Talleyrand was too controversial a figure to be accepted by the Swiss authorities and the risk of interception by French ships made a voyage to neutral Denmark equally out of the question. In the end he decided to seek refuge in the United States.

Thanks to the frantic appeals of his friends, the government gave Talleyrand a respite of three weeks to make his plans. There was no time for Madame de Staël to transfer money from Switzerland, but Narbonne arranged a loan for him against the security of his own property in the West Indies, and Lansdowne gave him letters of introduction to his contacts in Boston and Philadelphia. It was at least a starting point.

On 2 March 1794, Talleyrand set sail for America. 'At the age of thirty-nine I am starting a new life,' he told Madame de Staël,

> for it is life that I want. I love my friends too much to have other ideas; and then I wish to proclaim and proclaim loudly what I have wanted, what I have prevented, what I have regretted; I wish to show how much I have loved liberty and how much I still love it.[12]

'I felt a kind of contentment,' he wrote later. 'It seemed to me that in that time of almost universal misery, I would almost have regretted not being persecuted too.'[13]

1

The July Revolution

I T was 36 years before Talleyrand saw England again. This time his entry was triumphal. Less than two months before, while the coach of the deposed King Charles X rolled towards the coast and a safe haven in England, Louis-Philippe had been proclaimed king of the French, following the three-day insurrection – the July Revolution – when Paris had risen up in arms against the reactionary edicts of Charles X. Talleyrand's arrival at Dover on 24 September 1830, as ambassador of France – now a representative monarchy along British lines – set the seal on the legitimacy of the new regime and was treated as a great event. His ship was announced by a salvo of cannon; Lord Charles Wellesley, son of the prime minister, the Duke of Wellington, was waiting to escort him to London and his carriage, decorated with tricolour streamers, was greeted by cheering crowds along the route. 'When I heard the booming of the cannons from the fortress at Dover,' he wrote in his memoirs, 'I could not help remembering the time when, 36 years before, I had sailed from these same English shores, exiled from my country by revolutionary upheavals and chased from British soil by the intrigues of the émigrés.'[1]

During the tumultuous years that followed his expulsion from Britain, Talleyrand had played many roles. He had returned to France as foreign minister after the fall of Robespierre in 1794, helped by the money and efforts of Madame de Staël, whom he later discarded coolly, as he would discard many others in the course of his career. From the Directory to the Consulate, from the Consulate to the rise of Napoleon, he had been at the centre of events, never the leading player, but always a key figure behind the scenes. He had served as foreign minister through all the tremendous dramas of the Napoleonic Wars, only resigning office when Napoleon in his view betrayed the interests of France – first with the invasion of Spain in 1807, then with the campaign against Russia. It had been thanks to his good relations with the tsar, with whom he had been secretly corresponding, that it had been possible to achieve a peaceful transition to a constitutional monarchy when Russian troops reached Paris in 1814. And it had been thanks to his consummate skills as a diplomat at the Congress of Vienna that France had been saved from dismemberment by the victorious allies and had been able to take her place among the great powers of Europe again.

With the establishment of Louis XVIII (Louis XVI's younger brother) as a constitutional monarch, it might have been thought that Talleyrand's work was done. This was certainly the opinion of the king, who in September 1815 dismissed Talleyrand as his chief minister, offering him the face-saving sinecure of grand chamberlain instead. For the next 15 years Talleyrand watched French politics from the sidelines, spending long stretches of time at his magnificent chateau of Valençay, deep in the countryside of Berry. One of the lessons that he had learned from his impoverished stay in London was never to be a '*pauvre diable*' (poor devil) again, and during the years that followed he had enriched himself shamelessly under every regime which he had served. It was not unusual at the time for statesmen to accept inducements and rewards from foreign powers; it was the scale of his venality that shocked his contemporaries. 'When he is not intriguing he is trafficking,' wrote his arch-enemy Chateaubriand;[2] even his admiring biographer Duff Cooper admitted that Talleyrand's 'conduct with regard to money, from the beginning to the end of his career, was indefensible.'[3]

One reason why Talleyrand was content to spend long periods at Valençay was that after innumerable love affairs he had finally found happiness in his private life. In 1802, under pressure from Napoleon, he had married his mistress Catherine Grand. Beautiful and silly – 'one has to have been the lover of Madame de Staël to appreciate a stupid woman,' he remarked[4] – she had long been separated from Talleyrand when in 1815 he settled down to a life of quasi-domesticity with his niece by marriage Dorothea, Duchesse de Dino, daughter of the Grand Duke of Courland. Thirty-nine years younger than Talleyrand, she had acted as his hostess at the Congress of Vienna, and though gossip suggested that they were lovers the proprieties were always carefully preserved. In Paris Dorothea had her own set of apartments in Talleyrand's vast *hôtel* in the rue Saint-Florentin, and at Valençay she lived in a separate wing of the chateau. Married off at the age of 15 to a feckless and unfaithful husband, by whom she had three children, she had been separated from him for some years. They were briefly reunited in 1821 when she moved in with her husband for several months; she gave birth to a daughter, Pauline, later that year. Malicious tongues suggested that Talleyrand was in fact the baby's father and that her husband's gambling debts had been paid off in return for his presence at the appropriate time. Whatever the truth of the matter, it was certain that Talleyrand and Dorothea were devoted to one another and that the relationship, whether platonic or not, was central to their lives. The fact that Dorothea sometimes had affairs with younger men did nothing to break the link between them.

In 1824 Louis XVIII died, and his younger brother Charles X came to the throne. A Bourbon who had indeed learned something, Louis XVIII had tried to steer the tricky path between revolution and reaction, between censorship and disorder, and had to some extent succeeded. Charles X showed no such willingness to heal the divisions in the country or to recognise the achievements of Napoleon and the Revolution. Obstinately set on turning back the clock, he had had himself crowned with medieval ceremony, passed laws condemning sacrilege and increased the privileges of the Church and aristocracy. Talleyrand had not been particularly supportive of Louis XVIII's moderate policies – probably because he had been piqued by the king's dismissal of his services. But he was appalled by the path which Charles X was following, which would lead inevitably, he thought, to the downfall of the regime. He did nothing to precipitate the crisis he saw looming. But he positioned himself accordingly. He had always been on good terms with the Duc d'Orléans, head of the younger branch of the Bourbon family, whose salon at the Palais-Royal was a centre of progressive opinion. The duke had no more desire than Talleyrand to undermine the monarchy. But the fact that a royal alternative to Charles X existed made him a focus of liberal hopes, and as the king's reactionary politics grew more unpopular Talleyrand was seen more often at the Palais-Royal.

Charles X's appointment of the arch-reactionary Prince de Polignac as his chief minister in August 1829 removed the monarchy's last chance of coming to terms with liberal opinion. From then on, with the smiling serenity of somnambulists, king and minister moved towards their doom. The opposition was gathering its forces; the liberal press, indignant at the choice of Polignac, attacked the ministry with unprecedented violence. Sustained by his belief in the divine right of kings, Charles ignored the warning signs. His minister shared his faith: he claimed to have heard voices and that he had been visited by the Virgin. 'There is no such thing as political experience,' wrote the Duke of Wellington, no liberal himself. 'With the example of James II before him Charles X is setting up a government by priests, for priests and through priests.'[5] Significantly, the liberal paper the *National*, founded in January 1830 by Talleyrand's brilliant young protégé Adolphe Thiers, devoted a series of articles to the English revolution of 1688.

In July 1830 the storm broke. On the twenty-fifth of that month, exasperated by press criticism and his government's failure to obtain a majority in the Chamber of Deputies, the king issued the fatal ordinances that would bring about his downfall, dissolving parliament, reducing the franchise and, above all, suspending the freedom of the press. This last clause sparked revolution. On 26 July, a group of journalists, led by Thiers, issued a manifesto, denouncing the clauses as unconstitutional, and calling on the nation to resist. On 27 July, the presses of the opposition papers, issued in defiance of the ordinances, were destroyed by the police. Angry crowds spilled onto the Paris streets; that evening, as garrison troops moved onto the boulevards, the barricades began to go up. By 29 July, after three days of bitter street-fighting, Paris was in the hands of the insurgents. The tricolour floated above the Tuileries, and Talleyrand, watching the rout of the royalist troops from a window on the rue Saint-Florentin, turned to dictate a note to his secretary: 'On the 29th of July, at precisely five minutes past twelve, the elder branch of the Bourbon family ceased to reign over France.'[6]

What of the younger branch? While the fighting raged in the streets of Paris, Charles X's cousin, the Duc d'Orléans, remained discreetly on the outskirts, sending messages of loyalty to the king. It was to him that the deputies, alarmed at the popular fury and seeking to contain it, now turned. Son of Philippe Égalité, a soldier in the revolutionary army at Jemappes, he had all the qualifications needed for a liberal monarch. On 30 July, he was offered the post of lieutenant general of the realm; it was, as he knew, the first step to the crown. Urged on by his brave and ambitious sister, Madame Adélaïde, and secretly advised by Talleyrand, he accepted. The next day, before a huge and still volatile crowd, he was proclaimed lieutenant general from the balcony of the Hôtel de Ville and, holding an enormous tricolour, publicly embraced by the republican hero, Lafayette. The crowd, persuaded by the tricolour, dispersed. The three days of revolution, 'les trois glorieuses', were over.

The transition to a monarchy was quickly achieved. Two days later, having confirmed his cousin's appointment, Charles X abdicated in favour of his ten-year-old grandson, the Duc de Bordeaux. But Orléans had come too far to stand down now. The abdication was announced without reference to Bordeaux, and on 8 August, after intensive discussions, limiting and redefining the royal powers, he was invited to take the throne as Louis-Philippe, '*roi des Français*' – or, as he was known, the citizen king. King of the French, but not of France, he based his legitimacy on his claim to be the nation's choice.

From the moment Charles X had been defeated Talleyrand had been in constant touch with Louis-Philippe and had worked with him closely on the discussions leading up to his acceptance of the crown. Far worse than the most reactionary regime would have been a return to the anarchy of the French Revolution, while the idea of a republic, first tried in 1792, still carried hideous memories of the Terror. The best hope for stability, in their view, lay with a representative monarchy along the lines set out in 1814, and first envisaged by the constitutionalists in 1789. With Louis-Philippe's accession to the throne this aim had finally been achieved. For Talleyrand, after more than 40 years, the wheel had come full circle.

Order had been restored in France, but the new government's position, attacked by disappointed republicans on the left and angry legitimists on the right, was still precarious. A period of peace abroad was essential to calm the political passions at home. It was far from certain, however, that the great powers of Europe would recognise the new regime. It was true that Louis-Philippe was a Bourbon, head of the French royal family's younger line; it was true too that in accepting the crown he had managed to contain the spread of revolution. But Austria, Russia and Prussia, the so-called Holy Alliance, created in 1815 to preserve the principle of legitimacy in Europe, were making threatening noises; it seemed for a moment that they might combine forces to restore the monarchy of Charles X. The recognition of the new regime on 30 August by the British prime minister, the Duke of Wellington, did much to stay their hand. The subsequent appointment of Talleyrand, the most experienced statesman in Europe, as French ambassador to London, was a further source of reassurance. 'Since M. de Talleyrand is associated with the new French government,' the tsar was said to have remarked, 'it must necessarily have a chance of lasting.'[7] He knew that Talleyrand seldom backed a losing cause.

The respect which Talleyrand inspired and his close relations with the Duke of Wellington, whom he had known in Paris and at the Congress of Vienna, made him a natural choice to represent the new regime. At first he had been unwilling to undertake the task. He was 76, he said, too old and infirm for the responsibilities involved. But the entreaties of Louis-Philippe and his sister, the importance of securing Britain's friendship and the knowledge that no one else was so well qualified to do so had finally decided him. He had been influenced too by Dorothea's eagerness that he should accept the post. She knew how much he had missed being at the centre of affairs during the previous 15 years; she had adored the interest and excitement of being his hostess at the Congress of Vienna. In London she could once more exercise her social skills and escape the carping tongues of the Faubourg Saint-Germain, where her various lovers and her relationship with Talleyrand had made her a somewhat scandalous figure. For Talleyrand her presence was essential. 'I knew,' he wrote later, 'that I could rely on her great and fascinating qualities to support me and to win us the goodwill of English society, so well known for its exclusiveness.'[8] The conquest of London was a joint enterprise in which, politically and socially, Dorothea would be his second self.

With Britain's acceptance of Louis-Philippe, the other powers reluctantly followed suit. But the echoes of the three-day revolution had barely died down when a new crisis arose, still more threatening to the European equilibrium. Riots by Belgian nationalists, demanding freedom from Dutch rule, broke out in Brussels on 25 August and quickly spread across the country; by late September the Dutch garrisons had been driven out of most of the major Belgian cities and a provisional government had been formed. Their success was greeted with enthusiasm by left-wing elements in France, who saw the Belgian revolution as a flattering reflection of their own.

Originally belonging to Austria, Belgium had broken away at the outset of the French Revolution and had been annexed to France in 1795. In 1814 it had been added to Holland in the Kingdom of the Netherlands, the idea being to create a buffer state on France's northern frontier. The union had been uneasy from the first; the Belgians, Catholic and mostly French-speaking, resented the dominance of their Dutch-speaking partners, and their Protestant monarch William I. By driving out the Dutch garrisons and forming a provisional government they had effectively won their independence. But would they be allowed to keep it? The Holy Alliance, in accordance with its self-appointed obligations, was preparing to put down the revolution in its usual way; the French, on the other hand, were determined to support Belgium against foreign intervention. The British, meanwhile, were adamant that Belgium, with its strategically and commercially important ports, should not fall under French control. Europe once more trembled on the brink of war.

News of the Belgian revolution had already reached Paris when Talleyrand left for London, adding greatly to the complications of his mission. Like Louis-Philippe, an Anglophile who had spent years of exile in England, he was convinced that co-operation with Britain was the best way to defuse the situation. If the two countries could agree to the establishment of Belgium as an independent and neutral state, the interests of both would be protected and together they would form a strong enough bloc to prevent the Holy Alliance from intervening. Ever since his first mission to London in 1792 Talleyrand had main-tained that an alliance between the liberal powers of France and Britain, counterbalancing the autocracies of Russia, Austria and Prussia, was the key to peace in Europe; even at the height of the Napoleonic Wars he had always spoken highly of the British system of government. With the accession of Louis-Philippe this goal was finally in sight. But how many difficulties there were still to be overcome! 'Even though I hid them from others in order to keep up their courage,' he wrote in his memoirs,

I could not conceal them from myself. They were many, serious and of a double nature. On the one hand was France, where a barely established government, struggling daily for existence, was unlikely to inspire much confidence in foreign governments. On the other, I could not ignore the fact that though the Tory ministry had been prompt to recognise our revolution, they did not regard it with a very favourable eye, especially since the uprising in Belgium... These were the thoughts which occupied my mind as I travelled through the beautiful English countryside, so rich and peaceful, and arrived in London on 25 September 1830.[9]

2

Ambassador in London

TALLEYRAND'S appointment as ambassador to London had been welcomed by the great powers of Europe but it was greeted by a storm of criticism in France. It was impossible not to recall his chequered past. A former bishop, whose love affairs were notorious, a turncoat who had abandoned one master after another, a gambler who seldom missed a chance to take a bribe, he presented a coolly impassive face to the world; he was someone, it was said, whose expression would not change if you kicked him from behind. All this could be repeated, and frequently was, by the opposition papers of both left and right. 'What have we done?' demanded Victor Hugo indignantly. 'We have sent Talleyrand to London. Vice and unpopularity personified.'[1]

In Britain, where Talleyrand was regarded as an almost legendary figure, his great age was the chief source of comment. 'I never was so astonished as when I read in the newspaper of the appointment of Talleyrand as ambassador here,' wrote Greville.

> He must be nearer eighty than seventy, and though his faculties are said to be as bright as ever (which I doubt), his infirmities are so great that it is inconceivable he should think of leaving his own home, and above all for another country, where representation is unavoidable.[2]

Talleyrand may well have felt the same when he was debating whether to take the post. But the die had been cast and his enthusiastic reception on arrival had been an encouraging beginning. The Duke of Wellington came up from the country to give a dinner in his honour the day after he reached London and Talleyrand exchanged the tricolour sash and cockade he had worn in public for the silks and jewelled orders of the *ancien régime*. He might be the representative of a bourgeois monarchy but he would play the part with aristocratic style.

The city to which Talleyrand returned was very different to the one he had known before. 'London at first sight,' he wrote to Madame Adélaïde, 'seems much more beautiful; whole new districts have been built; the population has greatly increased; it now numbers fifteen hundred thousand souls – if you can so describe the egoists who inhabit it.'[3] (For Talleyrand, as for Napoleon, the British would always be a nation of shopkeepers.) One thing, however, had not changed: the Tory party was still in office, as it had been, with one short intermission, for the last 40 years. 'Naught's permanent among the human race / Except the Whigs *not* getting into place,' Byron had written in *Don Juan*. But the old structures were beginning to break down. The fear of revolution, which for so many years had checked any changes in the electoral system, was giving way to a growing demand for reform. The bill for Catholic emancipation, long resisted by the right-wing Tories, had gone through the previous year, dividing and weakening the party. The Duke of Wellington was still in charge, but the Whigs were waiting in the wings.

Talleyrand's main business was with the party in power, but this did not prevent him from renewing his contacts with the Whigs. London society, still dominated by the aristocracy, was relatively homogeneous, its membership defined by class rather than politics, and Talleyrand could mix freely with both sides. During his previous stay, when he was treated as a pariah in most quarters, the hospitality and support he had received from liberal figures like Fox and Lansdowne had been among his happiest memories. A new generation had now taken their place:

Fox's nephew, Lord Holland, was a leading figure in the party, as was Lansdowne's second son, the third Lord Lansdowne. (Lansdowne's first son, Madame de Flahaut's former lover, had died a few years earlier.) Linked by long ties of family friendship and shared political ideals, they welcomed him as one of their own.

The question of Belgium loomed in the background as Talleyrand began discussions with the foreign secretary, Lord Aberdeen, and with Wellington himself. But his first objective was to justify the actions of Louis-Philippe in taking the crown. 'I think,' he wrote to Madame Adélaïde,

> that the duke [of Wellington] is now completely convinced that the French uprising at the end of July was instigated by no one, that the public indignation was general, and that there was no question of any intrigue; that the Duc d'Orléans was forced by circumstances to accept the lieutenant-generalship of the country, and later the crown; that in doing so he was carrying out his duty and rendering a service to the whole of Europe.[4]

Talleyrand had always believed in the importance of women in diplomacy. Madame Adélaïde was Louis-Philippe's closest adviser in private: French caricaturists used to depict her as a puppetmaster pulling her brother's strings. In his letters to her, and to his great friend and former mistress, Princesse de Vaudémont, an intimate of the royal family, Talleyrand was able to bypass the foreign minister, Molé, much to the latter's irritation. His despatches to Molé were scrupulously correct, but the real issues of Franco-British policy were worked out informally between Louis-Philippe, his sister and Talleyrand – 'it's entirely between the king, you and me,' wrote Madame Adélaïde at one important moment.[5] The trust between the three was based on years of friendship, and whatever Talleyrand's record elsewhere it was one that he never betrayed.

On 30 September, the Duchesse de Dino arrived in London to take up her place as Talleyrand's ambassadress. She was also his private secretary-cum-counsellor, the only person, she wrote to a friend, to whom he could freely confide 'the plans, doubts, hopes and duties which ceaselessly occupy his ever-active mind.'[6] Her presence was all the more important since, apart from an able first secretary, Comte Bresson, he was ill served by his existing staff: two other secretaries, two attachés, a consul and a secretary to the legation. Lounging about the embassy, and sporting enormous tricolour cockades, they seemed, he wrote crossly, to have been chosen for their revolutionary sympathies; one, a professed republican, had even been heard to drink the health of Louis-Philippe – but only when he left the throne.

It would take time for Talleyrand to replace these unsatisfactory officials; meanwhile, Dorothea was a vital support behind the scenes, as well as the most elegant of hostesses. Now 35, she was still at the height of her attractions. 'She has a tremendous air of distinction about her,' wrote a visiting politician, Charles de Rémusat.[7] Thin, with aquiline features, a sallow complexion and jet-black hair, she was not conventionally beautiful at first glance. But her face was illuminated by her amazing grey-blue eyes, dark-circled and brilliantly expressive. She was a little short-sighted, which added a caressing softness to her gaze; her lips were full and voluptuous, and her voice, with its slight German accent, had an attractive hesitancy about it. The whole effect, thought Rémusat, was infinitely seductive, almost to a fault.

She and Talleyrand made an extraordinary pair. With his powdered ringlets, limping gait and death-pale wrinkled face he looked, it was said, like an ancient lion; he could have posed with Dorothea for a picture of youth and age. Few people questioned their unconventional relationship. British society had not yet acquired the virtuous tone of the Victorian era; the easy-going morals of the Regency had continued into the reign of William IV. 'A hint of corruption', as one biographer puts it, was part of the prevailing climate.[8] Talleyrand's cool and witty cynicism was equally in tune with the times, and Dorothea's charm and style disarmed most critics of her private life. 'I am very fond of Madame de Dino. She is always very good-humoured and is very agreeable company,' wrote the wife of the opposition leader, Lord Grey. 'Since she never says anything to offend me, I have nothing to do with the lovers she is said to have had. I take no credit from being different from her; mine is a very lucky case.'[9]

London society opened its doors, but it was far from certain that Dorothea would be accepted by the Court of St James's. It was not usual for a niece by marriage to act as hostess for an uncle, especially in such equivocal circumstances, and the queen, a stiff and virtuous German princess, was at first unwilling to receive her. Privately, the king had not a leg to stand on – the court was swarming with his illegitimate children by his former mistress, the actress Mrs Jordan – but he was very conscious of the respect due to the crown. It was only after the Duke of Wellington assured him that Dorothea had acted as Talleyrand's ambassadress in Vienna and had been accepted as such by the emperor and empress that he grudgingly agreed. 'Oh, very well,' he said. 'I will tell the Queen and you had better tell her too.'[10]

William IV was prepared to swallow the ambassadress, but even though his government had recognised the new regime he privately regarded Louis-Philippe as an 'infamous scoundrel' for having taken his cousin's crown. A bluff and breezy former sailor, he was notoriously outspoken – to the despair of his ministers – and Talleyrand awaited his first royal audience with some misgiving. Fortunately, his old friend, Lord Holland, was on close terms with the royal family: Holland's illegitimate son Charles (born before his wife's divorce from her first husband) had married one of the king's illegitimate daughters. No one knew better how to handle the eccentric monarch, and, on 6 October, the day that he was due to present his credentials, Talleyrand sent him an urgent note, asking him to call that morning: 'I have my audience at four o'clock.'[11] Holland, an ardent believer in Anglo-French co-operation, would have been only too happy to give his advice.

Dorothea's memoirs describe her uncle's seemingly casual preparations for the audience. His valet, she wrote, was already helping him into his court dress when he turned to her and remarked that it might be a good idea to follow the example of previous French ambassadors by making a short speech to the king: 'Let's see, Madame; would you mind jotting down a few sentences in your largest writing that I could use?' 'This is exactly what I did,' wrote Dorothea. 'He changed a few phrases in my draft, which I recopied while his decorations were being pinned on and he was being handed his hat and cane.'[12]

Talleyrand never liked to give the appearance of effort – *'surtout pas trop de zèle'* (above all, not too much zeal) was his famous advice to young diplomats. But it seems likely that he had already carefully considered what he was going to say – perhaps running it past Holland that morning – and that Dorothea had merely summed up his conclusions. The two worked so closely together that their thoughts were often interchangeable.

Composed in appropriately formal language, but obviously personal in feeling, the speech referred movingly to past differences between France and Britain: William IV would be well aware that he was being addressed by the former foreign minister of Britain's arch-enemy, Napoleon.

Sire, of all the vicissitudes I have been through in arriving at my great age, of all the varied fortunes of the 40 years, so rich in great events, with which my career has been mingled, none perhaps has so fully satisfied my wishes as the appointment which brings me back to this happy country. But what a difference between the two epochs! The jealousies, the prejudices, which have for so long divided France and England have now given place to feelings of esteem and enlightened affection. Common interests unite our two countries ever more closely. In foreign policy, England, like France, repudiates the idea of intervening in the internal affairs of its neighbours, and the ambassador of a sovereign unanimously chosen by a great people feels naturally at home in a land of liberty, and in the presence of a descendant of the illustrious house of Brunswick.[13]

Hidden within the speech's graceful phrases were two important political points. The first was France's commitment to the principle of non-intervention, with obvious application to the Belgian question; the second, more daring, was the reference to the 'illustrious house of Brunswick', a reminder that William IV, like Louis-Philippe, descended from a junior line. William's ancestor, George I, ruler of the Duchy of Brunswick-Lüneburg (Hanover), had been brought to the throne by Parliament in place of the rightful – but Catholic – Stuart heir; he was no more legitimate than Louis-Philippe. The king could not fail to see the parallel but showed no signs of taking it amiss. Perhaps he was impressed by Talleyrand's impeccably aristocratic – and non-revolutionary – manner; perhaps he had been talked round by Wellington beforehand. 'He received me very kindly', wrote Talleyrand in his memoirs, 'babbled some friendly phrases about Louis-Philippe in his bad French and told me how happy he was to hear that the popular [or revolutionary] clubs had now been closed down in Paris.'[14] His last words, Talleyrand reported, were '*Au revoir,* see you at Brighton' – an invitation to the Brighton Pavilion, the oriental palace created by George IV, was a special mark of favour.[15]

Talleyrand was well pleased with his address, which, as he wrote to Madame Adélaïde next day, had made an excellent impression in court circles. He hoped it would be widely reported in France; not only would it reflect well on Louis-Philippe's foreign policy, it would also help to refute the 'violent diatribes' against him in the French papers. But Molé, the foreign minister, who had no desire to give him favourable publicity, declined to release it to the press; it was only after Dorothea had intervened with Thiers that it was published ten days later in the *National* – by then too late to have much effect.

Relations between Molé and Talleyrand were going from bad to worse. Molé resented Talleyrand's special access to the king and what he regarded as the insulting brevity of his official despatches. When he decided to intervene in the Belgian negotiations by writing to Wellington directly – 'without, let it be said', wrote Talleyrand, 'informing me'[16]

– Talleyrand confided to Madame Adélaïde that he found his behaviour rather childish. Infuriated by these and other pinpricks, Molé offered his resignation to the king.

Nothing, he declared, could induce him to continue as foreign minister if Talleyrand did not follow his orders in the same way as the least of his ambassadors. No one knew better than he the respect and even deference that was due to Talleyrand's age and experience; but neither, he added spitefully, did he forget that Talleyrand had closeted himself with the banker Gabriel Ouvrard on his way through Calais.

Molé was hitting at Talleyrand's weakest point. Ouvrard, a famously corrupt financier, was an old associate of Talleyrand's. In the confused state of European politics, with one revolution barely over and another taking place in Belgium, there would be ample opportunities for Talleyrand to play the markets from an inside seat in London. Napoleon had called Talleyrand 'the vilest of speculators' and there was no sign he had changed his ways.[17] Louis-Philippe, however, preferred to turn a blind eye to such matters; Talleyrand's importance as a statesman far outweighed his dubious financial dealings. But he did his best to soothe his minister's ruffled feelings and the uneasy partnership was patched up for the time being.

The most positive aspect of the Belgian situation, now dominating French discussions with the British government, was that the principle of non-intervention, referred to in Talleyrand's address to William IV, was one on which both countries agreed. Like most of his compatriots, Talleyrand had resented the creation of a united Netherlands in 1814, which he saw as a deliberate attempt to keep France within bounds, reinforced by the building of a series of fortresses along the border. On Belgium's eastern frontier the acquisition of the former French territories of the Rhine by Prussia had been part of a similar plan of containment – or revenge, as French opinion saw it. In Paris, nationalist elements were urging Louis-Philippe to take back Belgium and to carry the message of the July Revolution to their French-speaking friends. But the king, like Talleyrand, knew this would be fatal: any attempt to annex Belgium would be strongly resisted by the other powers and Talleyrand made it clear that France had no such ambitions. The Belgian problem, he maintained, was a European question, best solved by Britain and France in conjunction with the other great powers.

From the first Talleyrand had established an excellent relationship with Wellington and Aberdeen. 'Lord Aberdeen told Lady Holland, who repeated it to me,' wrote Dorothea to Madame Adélaïde, 'that there was nothing more agreeable than treating of affairs with M. de Talleyrand, on account of his broad and simple way of seeing them, and of dealing with them in all his communications.'[18] So good was the understanding between them that when, at the beginning of October, the king of the Netherlands appealed to the British government for help in recapturing his Belgian territories, he was told that the question could only be decided after consultation with the French. Austria and Prussia, similarly appealed to, replied that they could only act in concert with Britain and thus, by association, with France. It was thought that the tsar of Russia – whose sister was married to the Dutch king's heir – was likely to reply in a similar vein. In less than two weeks of his arrival, Talleyrand had succeeded in placing himself at the heart of the negotiations over Belgium. 'It seems to me,' he wrote to Molé, 'that in obtaining this result between 26 September and 8 October, no time has been lost.'[19]

3

The Belgian Conference

T HE principle of non-intervention – the term was the same in French and English – put forward in Talleyrand's speech to William IV had become a convenient watchword for both the French and British governments. But this did not mean that they should do nothing, as Aberdeen made clear to Talleyrand.

> If it is established that the king of the Netherlands is incapable of restoring order to his provinces, it is nonetheless of the greatest importance to Europe that things should not continue as they are today. We cannot, any more than you, remain indifferent to what is happening. While maintaining the principle of non-intervention we must work together to prevent other countries, who fear the spirit of revolution will spread to their own territories, from taking violent measures which will lead inevitably to war. Could one not try, by wise counsels, to broker an arrangement advantageous to Holland and Belgium, in such a way that each, by making some sacrifice, could retain what was really essential?... By confining oneself to this friendly role, the independent spirit of those concerned would not be injured and no other country could take offence. All Europe concurred in the creation of the Netherlands in 1814; it would be strangely deluding oneself to think that if the break-up of the realm is complete, the peace of Europe would not be affected.[1]

Talleyrand might have commented that France had not concurred in the creation of the united Netherlands, which had been forced on her by the victorious allies. But he was never one for looking back. 'God gave us eyes in front,' he once remarked, 'in order that we should look ahead.' Belgian independence was now a fait accompli; the next step was to determine what form the new state should take. For both Britain and France, a constitutional monarchy along the same lines as their own was the natural solution. But who should be the sovereign, and how could the other powers be restrained from intervening on behalf of the king of the Netherlands – Prussia in order to keep the revolution from spreading to the Rhineland, Austria and Russia to maintain legitimacy and the status quo? These were questions that could only be solved by a conference of the five main powers, in which Britain and France, as the countries most closely concerned, should take the lead. So much was decided by the middle of October, but the place and timing of the conference was still unresolved.

Immediately the question of national prestige arose. The French foreign ministry, represented by Molé, was insistent that the conference should take place in Paris. Wellington, together with the ambassadors of Austria and Prussia, was determined that it should be in London. Their argument was supported by the news from Paris, where a series of violent riots, some in support of the Belgian revolutionaries, some calling for the death penalty for Polignac and his fellow ministers, had culminated in an attempt to storm the Palais-Royal on 17 October. 'I lost no time in following your instructions,' wrote Talleyrand to Molé on 24 October.

> I conveyed and developed your arguments; I tried every possible kind of persuasion... but their resistance has only been strengthened by the latest events in Paris. They see our insistence on having the conference there as a desire to discuss the Belgian question in the midst of a revolutionary whirlwind; and they maintain this opinion with the French newspapers in their hand.[2]

Secretly Talleyrand agreed with their reasoning, and having done the best he could, was happy to give in; he had no desire to display the instability of the new regime to foreign eyes. Meanwhile, it was important to defend the new monarchy in public and play down its revolutionary associations. When the Duke of Wellington, for instance, referred to the 'unhappy' events of July, Talleyrand took him up sharply. No doubt, he told him, the duke felt a natural sympathy for the deposed Charles X (now living in exile in Scotland). But he should be clear that the July Revolution, brought about by Charles's disastrous policies, was neither unhappy for France nor for the rest of Europe – with whom, he added meaningfully, his country had every desire to stay on good terms. The duke had hastily backpedalled, agreeing that he had only used the word in the limited sense suggested.

More outspoken was Princess Lieven, wife of the ambassador of Russia, Europe's most autocratic power, and a formidable figure in her own right. She had long ruled London as its leading diplomatic hostess, enjoying close if not amorous relations with many of the leading statesmen of the day – the opposition leader, Lord Grey, was particularly under her spell, and wrote to her each morning on heavily scented notepaper. She had not welcomed the arrival of Talleyrand – politically suspect from Russia's point of view and a powerful rival socially – and had been quick to denigrate him to William IV. 'The king asked me what I thought of him,' she wrote after Talleyrand's first audience. 'I replied that someone who had spent 75 years of his life intriguing was unlikely to forget his métier in his seventy-sixth.'[3] She was particularly annoyed that Wellington thought so highly of him. 'The Duke of Wellington has completely fallen for the charms of M. Talleyrand,' she complained.

> You can't imagine the conviction with which he maintains that he is an absolutely honest man, and that anything that's ever said to the contrary is pure calumny. The probity of M. Talleyrand seems to me about on the level of the wisdom of M. de Polignac.[4]

She went too far, however, when she took on Talleyrand directly. 'You can do or say what you will,' she announced in front of a crowded drawing room, 'but what has just happened in France is a flagrant act of usurpation.'

'You are perfectly right, Madame,' replied Talleyrand suavely. 'The only thing to be regretted is that it did not take place 16 years ago, as your master, the emperor Alexander, desired.' (The tsar on arriving in Paris had considered the Duc d'Orléans the best candidate for the throne – it had only been at the insistence of the other great powers that Louis XVIII was chosen in his place.)

'I have to say,' wrote Talleyrand, 'that from then on she no longer tried to provoke me and our relationship became very agreeable, although secretly she did everything she could to upset our political negotiations.'[5]

Dorothea had her own battles to fight. Lady Grey's good-humoured acceptance of her matrimonial arrangements was not echoed in all quarters. But she was well able to see off her opponents, and when one bold spirit asked her where her husband was, she coolly replied that she had not the least idea. No one dared ask the question to her face again. With Princess Lieven she was soon on cautiously good terms, though onlookers enjoyed setting one against the other. Dorothea had the advantage of her youth and beauty; Princess Lieven, sharp-tongued and commanding, that of her long experience of English social life. 'They are both professional talkers – artists, quite, in that department,' wrote the Whig MP Thomas Creevey. 'We had them both quite at their ease, and perpetually at work with each other; but the Lieven for my money!'[6]

Later the balance would shift, and even in her first few weeks Dorothea won her way into some of London's most exclusive circles. 'There are five or six houses to which I can take along my needlework and invite myself to dinner when I wish,' she wrote in her diary for October. 'This is something so rare that I must account it as a great success.'[7]

One place where Talleyrand and Dorothea were certain of a whole-hearted welcome was Holland House, the palatial house in Kensington where Lord Holland and his clever, magnetic wife Elizabeth presided over the most influential salon of the day. Devoted to the memory of Fox, Holland House had long been the unofficial centre of the Whig opposition and had greeted the July Revolution as a triumph for the liberal cause. Holland had first met Talleyrand when he visited Paris as a very young man in 1791, and except during the Napoleonic Wars, had been in touch with him at every stage of his political career. Twenty years younger than Talleyrand, he was perhaps his closest friend in England. Talleyrand's letters to him, preserved in the Holland House Papers, are written in tones of easy familiarity, beginning in English with 'my dear friend' or sometimes 'dearest' and signed with a scribbled 'T' or 'Talley', his nickname in the British press. Their friendship, important in personal terms, would soon become so in politics too, for the movement for parliamentary reform was gathering pace and it was uncertain how long Wellington's ministry would last.

The Tories were still in office, however, when the five-power conference in London began on 4 November. Meanwhile, more mob violence, in which the crowd had attempted to storm the fortress of Vincennes, where Polignac and his fellow ministers were awaiting trial, had triggered a ministerial crisis in France. Molé had resigned – no loss in Talleyrand's opinion – and a new, more left-wing ministry had been formed. None of this was designed to reassure the other foreign powers. Even the British showed signs of getting cold feet, and when Parliament opened on 2 November the king's speech mentioned the spread of disorder in Europe with ominous disapproval. The conference could hardly have begun under less favourable auspices, but Talleyrand refused to be cast down. The confusion following the change of ministries in France had left him a more or less free hand in opening negotiations. He was encouraged too by the enthusiasm with which he had been greeted when he rode in the state procession after the opening of Parliament. Dorothea described the scene to Madame Adélaïde:

I've just come back from the state opening... I must tell you straight away that when the coach of the French ambassador appeared a chorus of cheers and hurrahs and cries of 'Louis-Philippe forever! No Charles X!' burst out from the crowd and followed us from the House of Lords all the way to Bond Street. There were also plenty of shouts of 'Long live Prince Talleyrand!' and when I appeared wearing my tricolour cockade, everyone cried out 'A French lady!' and cheered me all along the way.[8]

For the general public, eager for reform, the July Revolution in France pointed the way for change in Britain too. Most people expected that the Tory government would introduce a few moderate measures of electoral reform, if only to silence more extreme demands. For Wellington, however, the British system was already perfect, as he roundly declared when the subject was raised in the opening debate: 'I am fully convinced that the country possesses at the present moment a legislature which answers all the good purposes of legislation, and this to a greater degree than any other legislature ever has answered in any country whatsoever.'[9] He sat down to a stunned silence. Even his most faithful followers were dismayed.

The repercussions of the speech soon made themselves felt. Government funds fell by 4 per cent. The duke was booed when he appeared in public, amid cries of 'No Polignac', and fears of rioting were so great that a state dinner for the king and his ministers at Whitehall had to be cancelled in case their carriages were attacked. On 15 November, in a debate over the civil list, the disaffected members of the Tory party united with the Whigs and independents to overthrow the government. Wellington resigned and the leader of the Whigs, the 65-year-old Lord Grey, became prime minister. A lifelong supporter of electoral reform, he would make the preparation of a Reform Bill the first item on his government's agenda.

On a personal level, Talleyrand was sorry to see Wellington go. The two men had known and respected one another for many years. But the

Whigs were as set as the Tories on avoiding war over Belgium, and considerably more in sympathy with the new, left-wing government in France. Talleyrand was sure they could work together well. 'This administration will be strong and will be favourable to us,' he told Madame Adélaïde.

> I have many social contacts with its leading members; they all speak well of our recent changes, which they agree were *demanded* by events; that is the phrase they use. They wish for England and France to act together in everything to do with the other powers; they regard the prosperity and strength of France as a necessity for the peace of Europe and speak of our king with great respect.[10]

Unlike the Congress of Vienna, which had been attended by their foreign secretaries, the great powers were represented by their resident ambassadors at the London Conference. All were seasoned diplomats, most well known to Talleyrand already: Prince Lieven and the Polish-born Count Matusiewicz for Russia, Baron von Bülow for Prussia, Prince Esterházy and the Baron de Wessenberg for Austria. (The Dutch ambassador, Baron Falck, and the Belgian envoy, Sylvain Van de Weyer, were in attendance but not included in the conference.)

The conference took place at the Foreign Office, with Aberdeen, as foreign secretary of the host country, presiding. But it was Talleyrand, the oldest and most experienced statesman among them, who set the tone. 'I am not here as the representative of France,' he said at the opening of proceedings. 'French diplomacy has no role here. I am simply a man of some experience, sitting down among old friends to discuss affairs in general.'[11] In this spirit the first decisions were quickly made, and a protocol calling for the cessation of hostilities between Holland and Belgium – 'without prejudice to future arrangements' – was unanimously voted that same day.

The Dutch and the Belgians had fought themselves to a standstill; apart from Antwerp, which the Dutch still controlled, the two countries had more or less reverted to their original borders. No serious negotiations could begin till the armistice – provisionally based on the frontiers existing before 1790, when Belgium had broken away from Austria – had been agreed between the two countries. Communications were slow: the semaphore telegraph only covered short distances; messages to The Hague and Brussels took over two and a half days to arrive and the deliberations on both sides might take many more. Talleyrand's first secretary, Bresson, and a British opposite number, Lord Ponsonby, were sent to Brussels as observers. In the meantime, the choice of Belgium's future monarch – no other form of government was contemplated – was the chief subject of discussion.

The most obvious candidate as king, in the view of all concerned, was the king of Holland's elder son, the Prince of Orange – a choice which preserved the principle of legitimacy while respecting Belgium's claims to independence. More liberal than his father, the Prince of Orange might well have made an excellent monarch, but the Belgians would have none of him. Strongly Catholic, they had no intention of accepting a Protestant king, and on 24 November the congress declared that the House of Nassau was forever excluded from the Belgian throne. A new candidate would have to be found.

This was the state of affairs when the new foreign minister, Lord Palmerston, took over from Aberdeen. Within two days of taking office he presided at his first meeting of the conference. His assessment of its aims was pragmatic. Since the union between Holland and Belgium had broken down irrevocably, the only way to keep the French from taking over Belgium – which, in his view, 'could not even be attempted without involving Europe in war'[12] – was to establish it as an independent and neutral state. His chief aim, throughout the conference, was to stop the French from gaining influence, or worse still territory, in Belgium.

Talleyrand accepted this in principle but pressure from public opinion at home made it important to seize what concessions he could. Belgium's independence was established but there were minor advantages to be won, first in adjustments of territory here and there, secondly in regaining control over the fortresses built along France's borders in 1815. Palmerston, by contrast, was determined to prevent all encroachments and was deeply suspicious of Talleyrand's intentions.

Talleyrand had great respect for Palmerston, whom he described in his memoirs as one of 'the ablest, if not the most able man of business' he had met with in his career. But he felt that he lacked the detachment necessary for a statesman: 'He feels passionately about foreign affairs... Every political question becomes a personal matter to him; and in appearing to defend his country's interests, he is almost always pursuing some private hatred or revenge.'[13] This underlying combativeness – later evidenced in his so-called gunboat diplomacy – would increase the difficulties of Talleyrand's task. Nor were things helped by Palmerston's lack of diplomatic graces. He never worried about keeping foreign dignitaries waiting: diplomats, he commented, had nothing to do except conduct business with the foreign secretary, whereas he had the whole Foreign Office to run. Even Talleyrand, despite his age and distinction, was once kept waiting outside his office for two hours.

Palmerston had never dealt officially with Talleyrand – or 'old Talley' as he called him – though the two had met in Paris two years earlier. Prince Esterházy, an old friend of Talleyrand's from the Congress of Vienna, gave a dinner at the Austrian embassy to introduce them formally; at the end of the dinner, after arguing who should go first, the three men left the dining room arm in arm.

It was a happy beginning to an often vexed relationship. Although both Palmerston and Talleyrand were committed to keeping the peace over Belgium, their manner of approaching things was very different, Palmerston brusque and abrasive, Talleyrand coolly polite whatever the provocation. Now almost 50, with lavish side whiskers, and a formidable reputation as a dandy, Palmerston was generally regarded as a great ladies' man; he was known in the press as Lord Cupid and had many mistresses to prove it. Dorothea, however, was immune to his charms; she resented his rudeness to Talleyrand and made no secret of her dislike. 'It is seldom,' she wrote,

> that a man has a face so expressive of his character. The eyes are hard and pale, the nose turned up and impertinent. His smile is bitter, his laugh insincere... His conversation is dry, though I confess he has a certain wit. He has on him a stamp of obstinacy, insolence and treachery which I believe is an exact reflection of his character.[14]

If Talleyrand shared her feelings he was far too experienced a diplomat to show it. The success of the Anglo-French alliance depended on Palmerston's goodwill. As long as he achieved his aims he was prepared to put up with any amount of bad manners on the way.

4

Social Successes

I T seems extraordinary that at the age of 76, and in the midst of the Belgian negotiations, Talleyrand had the time and energy to establish his social position in London as well. But he was brilliantly successful from the first, not only in the upper reaches of society, but also among the general public. There were daily reports of his doings in the London papers, and crowds used to gather every morning to watch him emerge from the embassy for his morning drive. He was frequently accompanied by his great niece, Pauline, now aged ten, and, to the delight of the English, by his spaniel Carlos; Talleyrand adored dogs and always had one or more in his entourage.

Sumptuousness, in the words of Lamartine, was part of Talleyrand's diplomacy, and the embassy in Portland Place was run on a magnificent scale, Dorothea privately complaining that it would ruin them. 'The rooms,' in the words of an admiring visitor,

> were done up with all the splendour of the great French aristocratic salons of the eighteenth century; the cuisine was perfection and the inexhaustible wit of the host and the amiability of the hostess made their receptions the most brilliant and sought after in London.[1]

Most of the guests, whether members of the government or diplomats, came from the aristocracy, though the visits of bourgeois French deputies from the new government occasionally lowered the tone; Dorothea complained of their ignorance and lack of social graces. No one could be more snobbish in private; of semi-royal birth herself, she looked askance on Lady Jersey, the doyenne of London society, because her grandfather was a banker, and once complained of being asked to dinner with one of Palmerston's current loves, a Mrs Petre, because she was a commoner. But she hid her prejudices in public and cheerfully donned a tricolour cockade on state occasions.

Conversation at the embassy was almost entirely in French; Talleyrand was never heard to utter more than a phrase or two of English, though he knew it very well. (One is reminded of de Gaulle.) But early nineteenth-century London was a famously cosmopolitan place, where knowledge of French – the diplomatic language of the day – was almost taken for granted among the educated classes. Talleyrand's bons mots, dropped carelessly into the hubbub of conversation, were endlessly repeated. He could often be silent in company but 'now and then' – observed the Duke of Wellington – 'he comes out with a thing you remember for all the rest of your life.' He quoted Talleyrand's reaction on hearing of Napoleon's death as an example: 'Somebody in the room at the time exclaimed: *Quel événement! Non*, replied Talleyrand, *ce n'est plus un événement, c'est une nouvelle.*' (What an event! No... it is no longer an event, it is only news.)[2]

Talleyrand's popularity in London was all the more remarkable in view of his earlier reputation. 'No name,' wrote Greville, 'was once held in greater detestation in England... He was looked upon almost universally as a sink of moral and political profligacy.'[3] For some the impression still lingered. 'He crawled past me like a lizard along the wall,' wrote the Duke of Devonshire's sister, Lady Granville, when she saw him at a state reception; having lived in Paris on and off for many years she had no illusions about his chequered past.[4] Nor was she best pleased at the success that Dorothea was having: 'I dined at Stafford House last night,' she wrote soon after her arrival. 'Lady Stafford has a sort of *engouement* for Dino. She can talk of nothing else, and her manner to her is affectionate homage. She can say nothing but "Is she not beautiful? Is she not interesting?"[5]

But even Lady Granville found herself seduced when Talleyrand came to call on her in Paris, where her husband was ambassador, while he was on leave there in 1832. 'Did I tell you,' she wrote to her sister,

> Talleyrand paid me a long visit on Wednesday morning. I never knew before, as Mr Foster says, the power of his charms. First of all, it is difficult and painful to believe that he is not the very best man in the world, so gentle, so kind, so simple and so grand. One forgets the past life, the present look. I could have sat for hours listening to him.[6]

It was this mixture of grandeur and simplicity which most struck those who met him and gave his company its special attraction. Added to this was the interest of encountering someone so intimately concerned with history – no one could be more fascinating when he wished. 'Still retaining his faculties unimpaired,' wrote Greville,

> and his memory stored with the recollections of his extraordinary and eventful career... his delight was to narrate, which he used to do with an abundance, a vivacity and a *finesse* peculiar to himself, and to the highest degree interesting and attractive.[7]

Nowhere was Talleyrand happier or more outgoing than at Holland House, with its brilliant cast of distinguished foreigners, artists, intellectuals and Whig grandees. Lady Holland, whose scandalous past – she had left her first husband to marry Holland – meant that she was not received at court, had created her own court at Holland House, where she reigned like a despot over her guests. Beautiful and domineering, she could strike terror into timid visitors; a London chemist was said to have invented a special pill for people who had been frightened there.

Talleyrand took her with a pinch of salt. 'She pretends to know everything, because it makes her look important, and when she doesn't she makes it up,' he once remarked, and when someone asked why she had changed the time of her dinners to the inconveniently early hour of five, said frankly: 'It's just to put everybody out.'[8] Like everyone else, however, he delighted in the gatherings at Holland House. Macaulay, a frequent visitor, captures the flavour of evenings in the long, panelled library, where guests would assemble after dinner and Talleyrand's anecdotes were among the star attractions:

> The last debate was discussed in one corner and the last comedy of Scribe in another; while Wilkie [the painter] gazed with modest admiration on [Sir Joshua] Reynolds' Baretti; while Mackintosh turned over Thomas Aquinas to verify a quotation; while Talleyrand related his conversation with Barras at the Luxemburg, or his ride with Lannes over the field of Austerlitz.[9]

Not only did Talleyrand find good company at Holland House, he also benefited from his host's position in the Cabinet – Holland was chancellor of the Duchy of Lancaster – to pursue his diplomatic aims. Some people thought Holland was taken in by Talleyrand. '[He goes] every evening late to Holland House, when everyone else is gone, and sucks Holland's brain for an hour or two before he goes to bed,' reported the Duke of Bedford to his brother, Lord William Russell.[10] But Holland shared Talleyrand's aim of ensuring good relations between their two countries and their confidence was mutual. Neither was much bothered by the niceties of going through official channels, a fact which could drive their foreign ministers to distraction, but though Palmerston occasionally exploded when Holland was particularly indiscreet, the interchange worked well for both sides. Nor was Palmerston above stooping to stratagems of his own. One of his ways of passing on information was to write privately to his ambassador, Lord Granville, forwarding his letters through the foreign ministry in France, where he knew they would be opened on the way. In this way important points could be made, without the loss of face involved in a formal confrontation between the two powers.

The refusal of the Belgian congress to accept the Prince of Orange as their king – the preferred solution of all the European powers – had thrown the question of the Belgian monarchy back into the melting pot. Meanwhile, the new French foreign minister, Comte Sébastiani, had come up with an alternative proposition and had sent over a special envoy to discuss it. His emissary was none other than the Comte de Flahaut, Talleyrand's illegitimate son by Madame de Flahaut – a dashing cavalry general, who had served as Napoleon's aide-de-camp at Waterloo. Talleyrand refers obliquely to their relationship in his memoirs: 'It was supposed,' he wrote, 'that the benevolent interest I had shown in M. de Flahaut's early career would make his presence agreeable to me in the current circumstances.'[11] In fact, this was far from being the case. Flahaut and his wife, an ambitious Scottish heiress, with many connections among the Whig aristocracy, had secret hopes of taking over the embassy themselves and were intriguing with their London friends to do so. Father and son were on uneasy terms in consequence, and matters were not helped by the proposal Flahaut brought with him: the division of Belgium between Holland, France and Prussia, with Britain taking Antwerp as a consolation prize.

Talleyrand rejected the idea indignantly. 'It did not need much reflection,' he wrote,

> to demonstrate how dangerous, mad, contrary to the establishment of a lasting peace and above all to France's real interests such a project would be. I recalled all it had cost France in blood and pains to expel the English from the continent in past centuries and I declared that for my part I would rather cut off my hand than sign any treaty which allowed them back. The extension of Prussian territory along our northern borders

was equally objectionable in my eyes. To my mind there was only one possible outcome that benefited France: the creation of a kingdom of Belgium under some prince or other who would be too weak to trouble us or even to garrison the fortresses that have been erected against us.[12]

The last sentence summed up his views on Belgium in a nutshell, and he repeated them more formally in his official reply. Flahaut went back to Paris with a flea in his ear – Talleyrand had no intention of giving up the embassy – and the idea of dividing Belgium was dropped for the time being. Sébastiani, a general who had served both Napoleon and the Bourbons, was a friend and former protégé of Talleyrand's and would prove far easier than Molé to deal with. The latter had tried to assert his authority over the ambassador; Sébastiani – on the whole – was happy to go along with his ideas. He knew that Talleyrand had the backing of Louis-Philippe and his sister, and shared their stated aim of 'peace at home and peace abroad'. His own role, a difficult one, was to keep the extremists in his government under control. Russia, in particular, was in a trigger-happy mood, with an army standing by in case the French invaded Belgium, and Austria, Prussia and even Britain had not ruled out the use of force.

On 29 November a revolution against Russian rule broke out in Poland; its savage repression by the Russian army shocked public opinion in both France and Britain. The immediate result, as far as the Belgian question was concerned, was to remove the threat of Russian intervention and divert the attention of Austria and Prussia, fearful of risings in their own domains. In Paris, however, the news of the Polish rising had an inflammatory effect. 'It is a second July revolution,' declared a young republican, Louis Blanc.[13] Riots broke out in the capital in support of invading Belgium and saving Poland. At the same time the trial of Polignac and his fellow ministers had aroused such furious emotions that the defendants had to be smuggled out by a back door in order to save them from the mob. (They were sentenced to life imprisonment, later commuted to exile.) Law and order seemed on the verge of breaking down altogether. 'This was a matter of great anxiety in Paris,' wrote Talleyrand,

> and this anxiety, as well as its causes, did not make the position of the ambassador of France in London very comfortable. It's not easy for a negotiator to assume a firm and haughty tone when at any moment he may be asked: 'Does your government still exist?'

'Nevertheless,' he continued, 'I refused to allow myself to be discouraged.'[14] The conference was moving towards the joint recognition of Belgian independence. It did not matter what monarch was chosen, thought Talleyrand, as long as Belgium's status as a separate and neutral country was confirmed. On 20 December, the principle of Belgian independence – the details to be negotiated later – was established in a protocol signed by all five powers. It was a triumph to have brought the legitimist countries, two of whose rulers were related to the king of Holland, to this point. 'I'm sending you the protocol of our conference, which has just this moment been signed,' wrote Talleyrand in a hasty note to Sébastiani that evening. 'The signature of the Russian ambassador, which you'll see there, is particularly precious.'[15]

Not unnaturally, the king of Holland was furious at the conference's decision. 'One cannot deny that he had good reasons to complain,' wrote Talleyrand,

> when one remembers that the Belgian provinces were ceded to him in 1814, in return for Dutch colonies [in South Africa and the West Indies] which England had taken for itself. It was up to the English to get themselves out of that one; as far as I was concerned, the only thing that mattered was that the Kingdom of the Netherlands, which had been put together out of hatred for France, had fallen apart, and was no longer sustainable.[16]

With the protocol agreed in principle, the five powers quickly settled the border between the two countries, following the line of the frontier between Holland and the Austrian Netherlands (as Belgium then was) as it existed before 1790. The only major stumbling block was Luxembourg. It had never officially been part of Holland, but the king of Holland was also Grand Duke of Luxembourg and as such one of the sovereigns of the German Confederation. The people of Luxembourg, however, had joined the Belgian revolution and Luxembourg was now occupied by Belgian troops. Talleyrand, eager to placate French public opinion, would like to have claimed it for France, or failing that for Belgium, but the king of Holland was backed by Austria and Prussia and he was overruled. So too was his attempt to reclaim the frontier districts of Philippeville and Marienberg, which had been lost to France after Waterloo, though he 'fought like a lion' to do so. 'At last,' wrote Palmerston after a debate which lasted for eight and a half hours,

> he was brought to terms in the same way that juries are – by starvation. Between nine and ten at night he agreed to what we proposed, being, I have no doubt, secretly delighted to have got the neutrality of Belgium established.[17]

The protocol, later known as the *Bases de séparation*, was signed on 20 January 1831. Even though he had failed to gain any territorial concessions, Talleyrand was indeed delighted. From now on Belgium was a neutral country along the lines of Switzerland, and the fortresses erected along its frontier were no longer a threat to its French neighbours. The other four powers too heaved a sigh of relief. The only discontented parties were the Dutch and Belgians, and as time would show they were not going to accept the arrangements made for them without a fight.

5

The Search for a Monarch

T HE declaration of Belgian independence was greeted in London
as a triumph for the Anglo-French alliance. Talleyrand's role as a
peacemaker and the guiding spirit of the conference was celebrated at a
grand banquet at the Mansion House at which he was the guest of honour.
Visibly moved by the warmth of his welcome, he proposed a toast to

the union of two great peoples who enjoy the rare happiness of offering
Europe the prospect of freedom protected by law and guaranteed by the
popularity of sovereigns who know all the advantages of peace and are
united in their desire to maintain it.[1]

'The thunderous and sustained applause which greeted this statement,'
writes one of his biographers,

was not so much for the words themselves... but for the man who spoke
them, a figure who, in his extreme old age, was expending what energies
remained to him in that pursuit of peace that was, as it had always been,
the most laudable passion of his life.[2]

In France reactions were more mixed. The king and his sister were
delighted by Talleyrand's 'great coup', as they called it, and Sébastiani

paid tribute to his achievement in the Chamber of Deputies. But a large section of the French public was furious that Belgium had been lost to France and felt that Talleyrand had sold out to Britain. Freedom of the press was one of the founding principles of the July Monarchy and the papers outdid themselves in abusing him. He was a Judas, a turncoat, 'the Satan of the Tuileries'. Talleyrand paid no attention to their insults. When asked his opinion of some particularly offensive verses he dismissed them with a witty phrase: '*La corruption engendre les vers*' (Corruption engenders verses/worms – the two words are the same in French).[3]

Meanwhile the problem of choosing a monarch for Belgium had not been solved. In theory this should have been the choice of the Belgian people, but as the conference's decisions had shown, the principle of 'non-intervention' was not an absolute term. Nothing could be decided without the consent of the five powers, and neither of the candidates favoured by the Belgians was acceptable to them all. The first, the Duke of Leuchtenberg, son of Napoleon's stepson Eugène de Beauharnais, was strongly opposed by France and Prussia: the last thing either of them wanted was a Bonapartist neighbour. The other, Louis-Philippe's second son, the Duc de Nemours, would have been welcomed by the French but was unacceptable to the British, as Louis-Philippe and Talleyrand were well aware. Nevertheless, when on 3 February 1831 the Belgian congress voted for the Duc de Nemours as their king, Louis-Philippe was sorely tempted to accept. Flahaut, sent to London to test the waters, shared Talleyrand's view that this would be disastrous. But it was only when Palmerston made it clear, in private letters to Lord Granville, which he knew would be opened in France, that Britain was prepared to go to war if Nemours accepted the Belgian crown that Louis-Philippe reluctantly climbed down. On 17 February, in the teeth of furious attacks from all sides, he refused the Belgian offer on behalf of his son. In putting the peace of Europe before his dynasty he made one of the bravest decisions of his career.

Talleyrand had always known that the choice of Nemours – in practice uniting France and Belgium – would never work, and had his own ideas on who the future king should be. His preferred choice, Prince Leopold of Saxe-Coburg, had the advantage of not being related to any of the royal families of the five great powers, though as the widower of George IV's daughter, Princess Charlotte – she died in childbirth in 1816 – he had links of sympathy with Britain. If a marriage could be arranged with one of Louis-Philippe's daughters, French interests would be satisfied as well. Forty-one years old, liberal-minded and intelligent, Prince Leopold had fought as a general under the tsar during the Napoleonic Wars, and was far more attractive and experienced than any of the other princes who had been suggested.

Talleyrand had already discussed the subject informally with Palmerston the previous December, reporting his conversation in a letter to Madame Adélaïde. The two men had run through the names of various candidates, Talleyrand rejecting Leuchtenberg, but intimating that Louis-Philippe would not insist on Nemours. 'It would be difficult for the other powers to accept him,' agreed Palmerston, 'but let us try to find someone else who can please everyone by making the right marriage.'

'What we call "everyone",' said Talleyrand frankly, 'in fact means you and us.'

'All of this,' he wrote,

brought us considerably closer to the subject of Prince Leopold and the possibility of him marrying one of our princesses, but it was Lord Palmerston who first suggested his name. I pretended to be a little astonished, as if the idea had never occurred to me before; but I gave the impression that I found the surprise a happy initiative. I promised I would write to Paris to report our conversation and get back to him.[4]

The seed had been sown, and discussions with Leopold and the other powers could begin. The Holy Alliance had no strong objections; even the Dutch agreed that any other candidate would be worse. The French government's first reaction was that Leopold was too pro-British; it would take some persuasion to convince them that a French marriage would redress the balance. But once the Duc de Nemours had been excluded they came to regard him as the next best choice, especially as the Belgians themselves seemed to welcome the idea. To bring so many different strands together called for long and complicated negotiations; they would pursue their course for several months as the small print was worked out and the division of debts and assets between Holland and Belgium was fought over. Leopold, who had previously refused the crown of Greece – newly liberated from Turkish rule – had no intention of accepting Belgium on unfavourable terms.

His marriage to the 19-year-old princess Louise d'Orléans would be more easily arranged. Royal families were used to dynastic marriages, which often turned out very well. Louis-Philippe was deeply happy with his wife, Marie-Amélie, the niece of Marie Antoinette, and Louise soon fell in love with the handsome, though not always faithful, Leopold. The fact that she was a Catholic – Leopold being Lutheran – was an important factor for the Catholic majority in Belgium, since the children, including the heir to the throne, would be brought up as Catholics.

Talleyrand was in the thick of these negotiations. Having lost his first secretary, Bresson, still in Brussels as an observer, he now had an admirable replacement in Adolphe de Bacourt, a provincial nobleman who had worked in The Hague for seven years and knew the current situation well. It was a perfect choice. It would be Bacourt, 30 years later, who edited Talleyrand's memoirs, and he proved to be invaluable from the first. He was 29 at the time of his appointment, good-looking (except for a tendency to baldness), with a slender figure and soft, dark eyes. Working closely in conjunction with Talleyrand and Dorothea, he soon fell under the ambassadress's spell. Whether they became lovers at this stage is not clear. Rumour certainly suggested so. 'They tell me you have been set on fire by those same bright eyes which touched me too in their time,' wrote Bresson to Bacourt from Brussels. 'I advise you not to limit yourself to a love as respectful as mine: to act has its advantages and life is short.'[5]

On earlier occasions Talleyrand showed signs of jealousy of Dorothea's younger lovers. But he seems to have accepted Bacourt quite happily, and their shared objective of steering France through troubled waters kept them close together. Revolution was once more sweeping Europe. In January and February 1831, a series of risings broke out in Italy and Germany, successfully suppressed by Austria and Prussia once it became clear that the insurgents could expect no help from the French government. The doctrine of non-intervention, in this case, was a useful cover for inaction. In Poland, however, the Polish and Russian armies were still locked in combat, and Talleyrand at least would have liked to try some form of mediation. 'Everyone today realises that a strongly constituted Poland would be the best barrier against the threat of Russian invasion,' he had written to Sébastiani in December. 'It seems to me that one could achieve this aim without going to war; the Cabinet in St Petersburg, if properly advised, might perhaps yield in time to our combined approaches.'[6]

Austria and Prussia, however, were caught up with their own problems, while Palmerston saw no point in making the attempt. Russia was too far away; he sympathised with the Poles but felt that they were fighting a lost cause. 'Considerations of humanity,' remarked Talleyrand, 'are only of very relative importance in England's foreign policy.'[7]

Closer to home and of more immediate urgency was the situation in Belgium. On 19 February, two days after Louis-Philippe refused the Belgian crown for his son, the five powers signed a further protocol in London, confirming and guaranteeing Belgium's independence, and appointing a regent until a new monarch was found. On paper matters had been agreed; in practice things were far less orderly. Antwerp was still occupied by Dutch troops; the Belgians had seized Maastricht in retaliation and neither showed any signs of abandoning their positions.

Talleyrand was disgusted with both sides. The Dutch were stubborn and resentful, the Belgians too disorganised to run their own affairs. In the long term he did not believe the new kingdom would last. 'Belgium will come to us eventually, but not yet,' he wrote to Princesse de Vaudémont.

> For the moment it's only a secondary matter... France must first be well and firmly established, and she can only become so by acting in unison with the great powers, who today *insist* on her participation; that's where I've managed to get things to in London. Let's not move from that position; it's taken me a lot of trouble to get there... It's far better to be in agreement with the great powers... and to be friends of the established order than of MM Van de Weyer [Belgium's representative in London] and Co.[8]

There were moments when the combination of the five powers seemed the only stable element in a shifting scene. Russia, Austria and Prussia had their own revolutions to deal with. In Britain, preparations for the Reform Bill were taking place against a background of violence: rick burnings in the rural south, armed gatherings in the industrial north. In Paris, a series of anti-clerical riots, during which numerous churches were pillaged or destroyed, had spread throughout the country, throwing the government into confusion and creating consternation in the money markets. 'There hasn't been so much agitation on the Stock Exchange since the July Revolution,' wrote Talleyrand to Sébastiani.[9]

Louis-Philippe was strongly opposed to violence; he was said to rule by the umbrella, not the sword. But behind the facade of a perfect bourgeois he concealed the will of a Bourbon and a capacity for survival that had seen him through many vicissitudes. He knew that his powers as a constitutional monarch were limited, but he was determined to break the pattern of near-anarchy which had marred the first months of his rule. The left-wing government was too weak – and too divided in its sympathies – to be capable of restoring order. On 13 March, thanks to some wily manoeuvring behind the scenes, he contrived to bring about its downfall, and a new and far more effective ministry was formed under Casimir Périer. A formidable politician, who managed to unite all parties in a policy of *résistance* to the forces of disorder, he would be largely successful in his aims.

Talleyrand was delighted with the appointment. 'After fifteen days of agitations, of upheavals and gloomy predictions about the fate of our beautiful France,' he wrote to Périer, 'the horizon has cleared, all our hopes are renewed and pinned to your name; it is with real joy that I saw it in the *Moniteur*.'[10]

For the first time since the July Revolution he had a prime minister he could respect. 'Périer,' he wrote in his memoirs,

> could never be called a wit; on the other hand he possessed in the high-est degree the strength and good sense of someone who has made his own way in life. [Périer was a successful banker.] By rare good fortune even his faults were positive qualities in the difficult situation in which he found himself. He was self-sufficient, a bit obstinate and sometimes got carried away; but all this gave the impression of a strong and indomi-table willpower and produced the best possible effect at a time when the weaknesses of some and the intrigues and violence of others needed firmly holding in check.[11]

He soon established a close relationship with the prime minister while remaining on good terms with Sébastiani, who had stayed on as foreign minister. The situation was complicated by the fact that Périer was determined to gather more authority into his own hands than previous prime ministers had done, and Louis-Philippe's powers – especially in domestic matters – were considerably curtailed. Nor did Périer get on with Madame Adélaïde; he resented her influence on her brother while she in turn thought his strong measures in restoring order – troops gathered round the capital, prosecutions for libel against opposition papers – were contrary to the spirit of the July Revolution. Talleyrand wove his way skilfully between these various personalities. He paid lip service to Sébastiani; continued his private correspondence with Madame Adélaïde and Princesse de Vaudémont (and thus indirectly with Louis-Philippe); and wrote directly to Périer whenever the occasion demanded. Périer welcomed his advice. 'Your profound and intimate knowledge of men and matters, my prince,' he wrote, 'will suggest the best ways to put our views across. Please write to me often; I wish to be well informed. I rely on your skilful and frank co-operation in everything.'[12]

It was no wonder that even the biddable Sébastiani sometimes complained of being sidelined. Talleyrand, on the other hand, was well content. 'I can only congratulate myself on my good relations with [Périer],' he wrote in his memoirs, 'and I acknowledge with pleasure that his presence at the head of affairs contributed greatly to the solution of those which had been entrusted to me.'[13]

6

The Eighteen Articles

A MONG the visitors to London in the spring of 1831 was the poet Alphonse de Lamartine. He had long been on good terms with Talleyrand, who had been one of the earliest to hail his first book of poems, *Les méditations poétiques*, in 1820. As a former diplomat as well as a literary celebrity, it was natural that he should call at the French embassy. Talleyrand knew he was a legitimist who had not supported the July Revolution, but this did not prevent him from giving him a warm welcome.

After dinner one evening he drew him aside on a sofa. Years later, in his *Cours familier de littérature*, Lamartine described their conversation. 'I'd like to talk to you alone,' said Talleyrand.

> You didn't want to rally to our cause… I don't insist. I think I understand you. You wish to save yourself for something bigger and more complete than the substitution of a nephew for an uncle on a throne without a base. You will arrive there. Nature has made you a poet; poetry will make you an orator; tact and reflection will make you a politician.

Talleyrand was looking beyond his own lifetime. He knew that the French Revolution had not yet worked its course and that in the long term the July Monarchy might not last. In 1848, in the first of a wave of European revolutions, Louis-Philippe would be forced to abdicate; Lamartine, by then a leading republican, would be one of the founders of the short-lived Second Republic. 'I know men's characters,' Talleyrand told him.

> I am 80 years old [in fact he was 77] and I can see further than the present time; you will play a great role in the events that will succeed it. I have seen the working of courts; you will see the very different movements of peoples. Stop writing verses, although I adore yours. It is no longer the age for them. Form yourself on the eloquence of Greece and Rome... I have seen the Mirabeau [the great revolutionary orator] of the past; try to be the Mirabeau of the future.

In one respect, said Talleyrand, he was more of a man than Mirabeau:

> Mirabeau was a great man but he lacked the courage to be unpopular... I've allowed my name to be exposed to every sort of insult and misin-terpretation by the crowd. People say I am Machiavellian and immoral. I am merely impassive and disdainful. I have never given dishonest advice to a government or prince, but I refuse to be dragged down with them. After a shipwreck a pilot is needed to guide the survivors. I have a cool head and I guide them towards a safe port; it doesn't matter which, so long as it provides a haven; what would become of the crew if everyone were drowned with the pilot?... They curse me in the French newspapers; they will bless me in years to come.

In choosing a great writer like Lamartine as his confidant Talleyrand was making his own plea to posterity. He knew that his politics were too tortuous for the upright Lamartine but he absolved himself from any charge of crime. (He was thinking perhaps of his supposed involve-ment in the kidnapping and execution of the Bourbon prince the Duc d'Enghien by Napoleon, a crime in which he always denied complicity.) 'There are many different ways for a statesman to be honest,' he told him.

Mine is not yours. I see that, but you will esteem me more than you think one day. My so-called crimes are the fantasies of fools. Why should a sensible man commit a crime? It's only for idiots in politics. Crime is like the tide; it comes back on itself and drowns you. I have had weaknesses; some people would say vices; but crimes? *Fi donc!* [1]

It is interesting in this context to read the verdict of a fictional criminal, the ex-convict Vautrin in Balzac's *Le Père Goriot*, on Talleyrand's role in public affairs:

A man who boasts of never changing his mind is a man who insists on always walking in a straight line, an idiot who believes in infallibility. There are no principles, there are only events. There are no laws, there are only circumstances. The superior man espouses events and circumstances in order to direct them... The prince at whom everyone casts a stone and who despises humanity enough to spit in its face all the oaths it demands, prevented the division of France at the Congress of Vienna: they owe him a crown, they throw mud at him instead. [2]

Le Père Goriot was published in 1834. In the midst of continuing attacks by the French press, Talleyrand must have welcomed this tribute from the greatest novelist of the age.

Périer's appointment as prime minister had done much to calm the situation in France. In Britain, where the Reform Bill was being furiously debated in Parliament, political unrest was growing. When the bill had first been presented to the House of Commons on 1 March it was considered so radical that not only the Tories but also the more timid Whigs were appalled. In fact, it was relatively moderate: less a democratic measure than a transfer of power from the aristocracy to the middle classes – very similar to what had taken place in France. But it aroused violent emotions on both sides. For its opponents it was the first step to revolution, for its supporters a blow for liberty and the reform of a chaotic electoral system. The first reading of the bill, as was usual at the time, had passed unopposed. All attention was now focused on the second.

Palmerston, like his fellow MPs (as an Irish nobleman he was not entitled to be a member of the House of Lords), was passionately involved in the debates that followed. Foreign affairs were all but forgotten. 'The discussions of parliamentary reform which are going on in the House of Commons absorb the ministers so much, by night and day, that it is impossible to speak to them about serious matters at this moment,' wrote Talleyrand to Sébastiani.[3]

When the vote on the second reading of the bill took place in the early hours of 23 March, the outcome was uncertain to the very last. The numbers were counted in an atmosphere of breathless excitement. When it finally became clear that the bill had been passed by one vote – 302 to 301 – a shout went up, wrote Macaulay, the new member for Calne, which could have been heard at Charing Cross. '*Notre devise est: Un me suffit*' (Our motto is: one is enough), wrote Palmerston, thanking Talleyrand for his congratulations.[4]

The reformers' triumph was short-lived. Three weeks later the bill was defeated on an amendment in committee and amid scenes of uproar in both houses the king was persuaded to dissolve Parliament. The election campaign which followed would last for 40 days, during which time, as Talleyrand complained, Members of Parliament would be scattered to all corners of the kingdom and Palmerston, as member for Cambridge, would have to return to his constituency. 'England at this moment,' he told Sébastiani,

is in the throes of an immense agitation, such as has not been seen since the revolution of 1688. The question of parliamentary reform engrosses every spirit, awakens every interest, and places the nation, so to speak, into two opposing camps. No one remains neutral, and everyone who belongs to a party abandons himself, and also his fortune to it without reserve... Ireland has added to its usual state the agitations communicated by England, and there are grave disorders in the south.[5]

One fortunate side effect of the election campaign from Talleyrand's point of view was a much-needed respite from the meetings of the conference. He was worn out by the intense activity of the previous six months and his health had begun to suffer as a result: he complained of rheumatism and feverish colds. Since the departure of Bresson to Brussels he had had only one effective secretary in the embassy, as opposed to the usual three employed elsewhere. Early in April Bacourt himself collapsed and was forced to take to his bed. On paper this was caused by overwork but perhaps there was an emotional element as well, in which his feelings for Dorothea played a part. But it left Talleyrand, as he complained to Madame Adélaïde, with all the work of the embassy on his hands. When Sébastiani, in a rare attempt to assert his authority, tried to impose 'one of his creatures' on Talleyrand instead of the new secretary – a certain M. Tellier – he asked for, it took a direct appeal to Périer before Sébastiani could be routed.

Staff shortages were only one of Talleyrand's irritations at the time. The brooding presence of Charles X, now living at Holyrood Palace in Edinburgh, was a constant source of embarrassment. Not only was he a focus for royalist plots but there were difficulties of etiquette to be dealt with. Even Queen Adelaide had to apologise to Talleyrand for accepting a contribution from Holyrood for one of her charity bazaars. Talleyrand had no wish to humiliate a man he had known for so many years, but it was important to uphold and strengthen the authority of Louis-Philippe.

Staying in Edinburgh at the same time, and another focus for intrigue, were the Duchesse de Berry and her 11-year-old son, the Duc de Bordeaux, who since the abdication of Charles X was regarded by legitimists as the rightful king of France. When the Austrian ambassadress (and niece of the Austrian emperor) Princess Esterházy told

Dorothea that she felt bound to seek an audience with the duchess before leaving Britain, Talleyrand did nothing to dissuade her. But he made certain that the princess, who was travelling through Paris on her way to Vienna, would receive a particularly warm welcome from Louis-Philippe and his queen. Since the duchess, knowing the princess was a friend of Dorothea's, had dismissed her coldly after only a few minutes, Talleyrand could be sure that he had won at least one advocate for the Orléans dynasty at the Austrian court. Meanwhile the duchess, who by no means regarded her son's exclusion from the throne as final, was beginning to make plans for a comeback. She would leave for Italy soon after in order to plot her return to France.

There were further problems of royal etiquette with members of the Bonaparte family. Here again Talleyrand felt the pull of former loyalties. 'If I believe now, as I did in 1814, in the danger of Napoleonic policies for my country,' he wrote in his memoirs, 'I can never forget what I owe the emperor Napoleon, and that is a sufficient reason for taking an interest founded on gratitude in the members of his family, though it cannot influence my political conduct.'[6] He had already encountered the emperor's brothers Lucien and Joseph in London, when he acknowledged them coolly but politely. He now heard that Napoleon's stepdaughter, Hortense, the former queen of Holland, was in England with her son Louis-Napoléon (later Napoleon III) and was seeking a passport to travel through France to Switzerland. The queen had a special claim on Talleyrand's good offices, since Flahaut, who had had a long affair with her before his marriage, was the father of her illegitimate son Charles; devotedly brought up by Talleyrand's old love, the former Madame de Flahaut, the child was thus Talleyrand's grandson.

For diplomatic reasons Talleyrand felt it better not to see the queen, but he sent messages to her through Dorothea, and managed to obtain the necessary papers for her journey. He used as his intermediary his old friend, the Comte de Montrond, who since his arrival in London had been going to and fro from France to England on confidential missions for him. Montrond, a corrupt and witty figure, who had first known Talleyrand under the Directory, had served as his unofficial agent – some said his jackal – ever since. Permanently short of money, he received a retainer from the French foreign ministry as well as picking up crumbs from Talleyrand's table and gambling for high stakes in the London clubs. Palmerston recalled how Montrond would wait in a coach outside the Foreign Office, ready to take orders for Talleyrand's stockbroker when the ambassador emerged from the conference, primed with the latest inside information.

Dorothea, who regarded Montrond as Talleyrand's evil genius, detested him and complained of his frequent visits to the embassy. She was jealous of his 40-year friendship with Talleyrand, and felt he reflected the worst side of Talleyrand's character. In this she may well have been right. A friend once asked Talleyrand, in Montrond's presence, to explain the basis of their relationship. 'If you wish to know,' answered Talleyrand, 'I should say that I am fond of Montrond because he has so few scruples.' 'You should also know,' said Montrond, 'that I, for my part, am fond of Talleyrand because he has no scruples at all.'[7] Their enemies suggested that the two deserved each other.

On 24 June 1831, after a hard-fought election in which the Whigs were returned to office with a greatly increased majority, the long-awaited Reform Bill was reintroduced in the House of Commons. This time it was passed by a majority of 136 votes on its second reading, but the struggle to get it through both houses would continue for another year and in the process bring the country to the brink of revolution. In his memoirs Talleyrand refrained from commenting on the debate. 'It would be straying from my subject,' he wrote, 'to enter into the details of the great measure destined to have such a grave influence on the future of England.'[8] But he must have remembered the opening stages of the French Revolution, when the moderate reforms envisaged by the constitutionalists had opened the way to the Terror and the downfall of the monarchy. For the opponents of the bill, and even at times the

Whigs themselves, the example of France was a constant reminder of the perils of reform.

Palmerston had been one of the casualties of the general election. His constituency, Cambridge, had rejected him in favour of a Tory candidate; there were too many clergymen in the university, he complained. A seat was quickly found for him elsewhere, ironically one of those that were due to be disenfranchised under the new bill, and with the election safely behind him he was able to turn his attention to foreign affairs again.

On 4 June, after long discussions in the Belgian congress, Leopold of Saxe-Coburg had been elected as king of the Belgians by an overwhelming majority. A deputation from Brussels came over to London to offer him the throne. A series of meetings between Leopold, the deputies and representatives of the five powers then followed, many of them conducted at the French embassy, where Talleyrand, who had collapsed from overwork (and also, he added, from irritation with the 'tergiversations' of the Belgian deputies), presided from his bed. But it was Leopold, not his deputies, who threw a spanner in the works. Acting like a ruling monarch before he became one, he refused to accept the Belgian crown unless the supposedly irrevocable frontiers established by the *Bases de séparation* (20 January) were altered to include Luxembourg and a number of other areas demanded by his subjects. Fearing his refusal might precipitate the creation of a Belgian republic and worse still spark off a general revolution, the conference reluctantly agreed to renegotiate its terms. A new protocol, known as the Eighteen Articles (24 June), made a number of important concessions in Belgium's favour, including leaving Luxembourg in Belgian hands. This was far from satisfactory to the Dutch, who protested vigorously at the changes, but since none of the other powers were prepared to back them it was assumed they would eventually fall in line.

Talleyrand had gone along with these arrangements. The prospect of a republican and possibly revolutionary Belgium alarmed him as much as it did the other powers. But he also had to deal with public opinion at home, where, even though Leopold would be marrying a French princess, there were many who regarded him as too pro-British. It was important to soothe their ruffled feelings. Thus, when Leopold, in accepting the crown from the Belgian delegation on 26 June, spoke of his close relations with Britain, Talleyrand was seriously displeased that he had not – as Talleyrand had suggested – mentioned those with France as well.

Leopold hastened to put things right. In speaking of Britain, he explained to Talleyrand, he had been talking of his past (as the husband of Princess Charlotte). He intended to make a positive reference to France – 'in the words your colleagues tell me come from you' – when he addressed the conference the next day. Meanwhile, knowing the importance of the relationship between their two countries, he had made a formal statement to the Belgian delegation:

> That I knew that the present arrangements had been described in some newspapers as hostile to France; that nothing could be further from the truth; that I had been on intimate terms with the family now reigning there for many years; that there were few countries I knew better than France, having stayed there frequently since my early youth; and that far from being hostile to France I regarded her as an ally, as important as she was useful, to Belgium.[9]

Since Leopold's statement was released to the press the following day Talleyrand was forced to be content. 'The Belgian question seems as well presented as it could be,' he told Sébastiani, 'and I think the king's government should be in a position to counter any attacks on the subject.'[10] On 21 July, amid general rejoicing, Leopold made his so-called 'Joyous Entry' into Brussels and was sworn in as king of the Belgians. (As with Louis-Philippe in France, he would rule as king of the people, not the country.) It seemed as though the Belgian question had finally been put to bed. It had been an almost interminable process. Looking back on his account of the negotiations in his memoirs, Talleyrand accepted that he might have quoted from the documents concerned at too much length. He had done so, he explained,

> with the double aim of clarifying the various points with which I have had to deal and of instructing any young diplomat into whose hands these souvenirs may one day fall, that patience is one of the first principles of the art of negotiation.[11]

His own had been more or less exhausted by the Belgian delegation; an amusing exchange recorded by Lord Holland captures his mood:

> Talleyrand, when told that the new King Leopold's choice of prime minister lay between two of the deputies lately in England and Mr le Hon, said he hoped it might be Mr le Hon. And why? said someone in surprize. Car je ne le connais pas [because I don't know him] said Talleyrand.[12]

7

French Troops in Belgium!

⌣

'ALWAYS dress slowly when you are in a hurry' was one of
Talleyrand's best-known maxims.[1] He did so even when he wasn't.
Dressing each morning was a ceremonial affair – almost a *levée* in the
old royal sense. We catch a glimpse of the process in the journal of the
diarist Thomas Raikes:

> I was rather amused today at Whites with [the Earl of] Sefton's descrip-
> tion of his visit this morning to Prince Talleyrand. He is very intimate
> with him and is received at all hours... This morning he was ushered
> into the dressing room of this celebrated octogenarian, who was under
> the hands of two *valets de chambre*, while a third, who was training for
> the mysteries of the toilette, stood looking on at attention to perfect
> himself in his future duties. The prince was in a loose flannel gown,
> his long locks (for it is no wig), which are rather scanty as may be
> supposed, were twisted and *crêpus* with the curling iron, saturated
> with powder and pomatum, and then with great care arranged into
> those snowy ringlets which have been so much known and remarked
> all over Europe. His under attire was a flannel pantaloon, loose and
> undulating, except in those parts which were restrained by the band-
> ages of the iron bar which supports the lame leg of this celebrated *cul
> de jatte* [cripple].[2]

Talleyrand applied the same stately pace to the business of the day, which began each morning with an hour-long consultation with his chef – 'our dinners form an epoch in the gastronomic history of London,' wrote Dorothea to a friend – and ended as often as not with a late-night game of whist at the Travellers Club, of which, like other foreign ambassadors, he was an honorary member. (In 1832, when the club moved to its present premises in Pall Mall, a handrail was added to the mahogany bannister especially for the benefit of the limping Talleyrand.)

Talleyrand's deliberately unhurried approach – '*surtout pas trop de zèle*' – had seen him through the long negotiations over Belgium. But he hardly had a moment to savour their success when a new drama blew up. Ever since the protocol of 20 June, revising the terms of the *Bases de séparation*, the king of Holland had been fulminating against the concessions made to Belgium. On 4 August he rejected the terms of the armistice; the following day a Dutch army of 36,000 men, led by the Prince of Orange, invaded Belgium. The Belgian army, disorganised and unprepared, was driven back to Louvain, which Leopold, fighting bravely at the head of his troops, was forced to abandon to the Dutch. In desperation he appealed for help from France and Britain. The French acted quickly; while the British were still assembling a naval squadron, their army had already crossed the frontier and marched to the defence of Brussels. They reached the capital before the Dutch, who then withdrew behind their borders, but continued to occupy Antwerp and maintain a threatening presence on the frontier.

French troops in Belgium! The conference was thrown into consternation. Talleyrand himself was completely taken by surprise, and was left for ten days without any instructions from his government. But neither he nor the other powers wished to make the incident a cause for war, and it was not too difficult to persuade them to issue a joint protocol condemning the Dutch action and legitimising the use of French troops for a limited time. For a moment, however, the future of Belgium hung in the balance and though he does not refer to it in his memoirs, Talleyrand was briefly tempted by the idea – which he had so strongly rejected earlier – of partitioning the country between Holland, France and Prussia. He never took it further; he knew that the British would then demand control of Antwerp and the prospect of giving them a foothold on the mainland was unthinkable. Nothing revealed his feelings – as well as his scepticism about Belgium's future – more clearly than a conversation described by Princess Lieven in a letter to her husband's foreign minister, Nesselrode.

The scene was the French embassy. Talleyrand, as was his custom after dinner, was drinking coffee at a little table in the corner of the salon when the princess came to join him. The two began to talk of Belgium and Talleyrand asked her what she thought about the matter. The ensuing dialogue – so she tells us – went as follows:

Me. – That you've taken a lot of trouble over something that will never last.

Prince T. – Ah! You think so?

Me. – And you, my prince?

Prince T. – I hope so.

Me. – What! Do you really think your Belgian kingdom and your Belgian king...

Prince T. – Won't last. Look, it's not a proper country. Two hundred protocols will never make a nation; Belgium has never been a proper country; it won't hold together.

Me. – All right! But afterwards, what?

Prince T. – You tell me.

Me. – Oh! If you want my opinion here it is: either Belgium to Holland or Belgium divided.

Prince T. – All right. Let's divide it; it'll help to pass the evening; you arrange it.

Me. – Nothing could be easier; we need to keep everybody happy.

Prince T. – Who's everybody?

Me. – I'll tell you who it isn't; neither us nor Austria.

Prince T. – Well then! Who's left?

Me. – You, a little; Holland a lot; Prussia probably; and then...

Prince T. – And then what?

Me. – Oh! Something for England. Antwerp for instance...

Talleyrand's well-known calm forsook him. Banging his stick on the floor, and hitting the table so hard that the cups rattled and everyone looked round, he shouted:

'Antwerp, Antwerp to England! Do you realise that what you're saying is revolting? What! England on the continent! Madame, as long as France exists, however reduced she may be, we will not, we cannot have England on the continent. You revolt me; the thing's impossible; what you're suggesting is abominable.'

'All right, my prince; let's not give her anything; it's all the same to me,' said the princess.

Talleyrand quickly recovered himself: 'Come! Come! I see you're joking.'

'Ah, so you've only just discovered it,' replied the princess gaily, and after a few more pleasantries they moved off to the whist table.[3]

Since the very beginning of his career Talleyrand had never wavered in his belief that an alliance between France and Britain was the key to peace in Europe. With France's emergence as a constitutional monarchy this conviction had become even stronger. 'We must try to establish closer ties with those countries in which civilisation has made the greatest advance, for it is with these that we have the most in common,' he had written to Sébastiani when he became foreign minister.

This leads us naturally to think of England... The other powers still pretend to rule by divine right, but France and England no longer think in such terms. Those powers support their right by the force of their cannon, but the English and ourselves are supported by public opinion and by principles. Such principles are of universal appeal, while the range of cannon is limited.[4]

Talleyrand's admiration for Britain and its institutions was genuine, but it was always a love–hate relationship. The memory of centuries of war and invasion lay deep in the French psyche. On the British side too old attitudes died hard. Both Palmerston and Talleyrand were convinced of the importance of the Anglo-French alliance. Palmerston knew France well; he spoke excellent French; he had rejoiced at the triumph of liberalism brought about by the 1830 revolution. But the Napoleonic Wars were only 16 years behind them, and his first instinct on hearing of the Dutch invasion was that the French must have something to do with it. 'Here's a pretty escapade by the king of the Netherlands,' he wrote to Granville in Paris. 'I wonder what's bitten him; we're inclined to suspect the French.'[5]

Could his suspicions have been justified? Had Talleyrand encouraged the Dutch to break the armistice in order to get better terms, and as a ploy to bring French troops into Belgium? It has been suggested – though with no supporting evidence – by one historian that this was indeed the case and that Talleyrand received a considerable sum of money from the Dutch to use his influence on their behalf. It would not have been out of character – his career was full of similar arrangements – and Louis-Philippe's daughter, when she became queen of the Belgians, openly accused him of having accepted a bribe from the king of Holland. Amid all the foreign honours heaped on Talleyrand, it is significant he never received one from the Belgians. On the other hand, Talleyrand was committed to a peaceful solution of the Belgian question and, since he had taken so many pains to achieve it, it seems strange that he should risk disrupting it.

Meanwhile, his task in London was made harder by the fact that, whereas the other powers were insisting that the French troops should leave Belgium once the Dutch had withdrawn, public opinion in France was demanding that they remain there till they had demolished at least some of the fortresses erected against them by the allies in 1815. For Talleyrand this was of minor importance: the fortresses would fall into disuse naturally once Belgium's neutrality was established. For many, however, the fortresses were symbols of France's humiliation after Waterloo: the destruction of even a token number would help to restore the nation's morale. Sébastiani, as a former Napoleonic general, was especially attracted by this view. Talleyrand knew the idea would never work; having erected the fortresses as a defence against France in the first place the other powers would never allow the French to have a say in their destruction. The French foreign ministry, he complained, behaved as if the rest of Europe did not exist.

Palmerston, of course, was having none of it. The French, he declared, had no more right to decide which border fortresses should be razed than a housebreaker had to choose which bolts and bars in your house should be removed. Their demolition could not even be considered till the French had evacuated Belgium. Using his favourite device of writing to his ambassador in Paris care of the French foreign ministry, he made sure his opinions were known. His formal refusals to Talleyrand in London were backed by forthright threats in his letters to Granville. 'One thing is certain,' he wrote on 17 August, 'the French must get out of Belgium, or we will have a general war, and war in a given number of days.'[6]

Fortunately, the rest of the British Cabinet took a less belligerent stance. Thanks to the peaceable influence of Grey and Holland, to the goodwill of the other powers and to Talleyrand's skilful handling of all concerned, above all his own foreign ministry, confrontation was avoided. On 10 September, to the vast relief of all parties, the French withdrew their forces from Belgium, Talleyrand in the meantime having obtained informal assurances that a number of the fortresses would be destroyed. French face had been preserved, and a new round of negotiations between Holland and Belgium could begin. After Leopold's defeat at Louvain, it was clear that the Eighteen Articles would have to be revised.

It had been a hectic time for Talleyrand: 'a bit too crowded for my age and strength', he admitted.[7] The conference's meetings often lasted late into the night, and to add to the usual burden of work and entertaining were the celebrations surrounding William IV's coronation, which took place on 8 September. The king, who had succeeded George IV, his brother, 14 months earlier, had been reluctant to have an elaborate coronation but his government had insisted, and the diplomatic corps was expected to play its role. 'The ceremony, which was very beautiful, was also very tiring,' wrote Talleyrand. 'One had to be at Westminster Abbey at 8.30 in the morning and stay there till 4.30 in the afternoon; then in the evening there was a grand dinner at the Foreign Office.'[8]

The Foreign Office dinner was followed three days later by a banquet at St James's Palace at which the leading foreign diplomats were again expected to be present. On this occasion the king, who had drunk freely, was in an exceptionally jovial mood. Greville records the scene:

> After dinner he made a long, rambling speech in French, and ended by giving as 'a sentiment,' as he called it, 'The land we live in.' This was before the ladies left the room. After they were gone he made another speech in French, in the course of which he travelled over every variety of topic that suggested itself to his excursive mind, and ended with a very coarse toast and the words 'Honi soit qui mal y pense.' Sefton, who told it to me, said he never felt so ashamed; Lord Grey was ready to sink into the earth; everybody laughed of course, and Sefton, who sat next to Talleyrand, said to him, 'Eh bien, que pensez-vous de cela?' With his unmoved, immovable face he answered only, 'C'est bien remarquable.'[9]

Dorothea had her share of royal ordeals. The queen's drawing room next day, she complained, was so crowded and long-drawn-out that the ambassadresses of Mexico, Brazil and Spain successively fainted from the heat. As a result of this reduction in their ranks the remaining diplomatic ladies were obliged to make a greater social effort than before. Princess Lieven, however, had her own ideas:

She sat herself boldly on the steps of the throne, and from there went through the king's room to find lunch. She then came back and told us that she was neither tired nor hungry. She might have been tempted to add that our legs ought to be rested because hers were and our stomachs filled by knowing that hers was satisfied.[10]

Talleyrand had never been happy with the French embassy in Portland Place, inherited from his predecessors under Charles X. Tall and dark, its reception rooms were on the first floor and Talleyrand found the staircase increasingly hard to climb. At the beginning of October, he and Dorothea moved to a new and larger building at 25 Hanover Square – today the handsome eighteenth-century mansion on the south-west corner of the square has a blue plaque recording his stay. The great advantage of the house, which they had rented from Lord Grey, was that Talleyrand's bedroom was on the ground floor. As much for receiving as for sleeping, it was a huge, high-ceilinged room, rich with tapestries, paintings, books and sculptures; Talleyrand's narrow bed, at the back of the room, was the only spartan touch. The other main rooms – also on the ground floor – were furnished in a similarly splendid style and receptions at the new French embassy were more magnificent than ever. The expense of entertaining in London, however, was alarming. 'You would never believe how much we are spending here,' wrote Dorothea to a friend, 'or how stingy the Ministry of Foreign Affairs has been.'[11]

While Talleyrand and Dorothea were moving house in London, events in Paris had taken a dramatic turn. On 8 September, Warsaw fell to the Russians; the brutal massacre that followed dismayed and shocked the rest of Europe. The news reached Paris on 15 September, giving rise to violent demonstrations by the left. From 16 to 19 September the city was in state of anarchy. 'The journals in London are full of the most terrifying news from Paris,' wrote Talleyrand to the Princesse de Vaudémont. 'Nothing here has caused so much anxiety in every walk of life since the events of July.[12] The situation was gradually brought under control, but it was not easy, he complained, to demand concessions from other governments while his own was in daily danger of being overthrown.

Talleyrand had always been respected – and lionised – by both Whigs and Tories during his stay in London. But the presence of French troops in Belgium had triggered a strong reaction among the hard-line members of the Tory party. Their suspicions lingered, even after the army had withdrawn, especially since a number of French officers had remained behind to train the Belgian troops. There had been rumblings in *The Times* (a Tory paper) about France's creeping encroachments, and on 30 September, in a debate on Belgium in the House of Lords, the Marquess of Londonderry (half-brother of Castlereagh, foreign secretary at the Congress of Vienna) launched a violent attack on Talleyrand himself. 'It could not be denied,' he is reported by *The Times* as saying,

that France was trying by every means in her power to undermine our influence and make us truckle to her ascendancy... The wily politician who represented that country here was no sooner beaten from one post [the evacuation of French troops] than he burrowed himself into another [using French officers to train the Belgian army]... He [Londonderry] did not think there was a person in the world with a character like to that of the individual in question... That individual had been first secretary to Napoleon; he had been minister to Charles X... he had been everything by turns. To see all our ministers running, one after another, to consult this individual, had created a degree of disgust which, he must say, he thought very natural... If the noble lords desired to know the grounds upon which he had formed his opinion of Prince Talleyrand's character, he would refer them to a memorial which this individual had addressed to the First Consul, dated the 15th Brumaire, year 11.[13]

(No biographer of Talleyrand has yet discovered this document.)

Londonderry's attack aroused protests from both sides of the House. Lord Goderich, speaking for the government, rebuked him for his 'imprudent, indiscreet and unjustifiable language' about the ambassador of a friendly power, pointing out the unfairness of raking up past actions taken 'when circumstances in France were so different that no man could act as his reason or inclination suggested.'[14] Holland too spoke up strongly for his old friend. But the noblest tribute came from the Tory benches, from the Duke of Wellington himself. In a speech interrupted by cheering from both parties he reminded Londonderry of the high esteem in which his 'deceased relative', Lord Castlereagh, had held Talleyrand at the Congress of Vienna. He himself, he continued,

> had no hesitation in saying that both at that time and in every one of the great transactions which took place then and in which he had been engaged with Prince Talleyrand since... no man could have conducted himself with more firmness and ability with regard to his own country, or with more uprightness and honour in all his communications with the ministers of other countries than Prince de Talleyrand. They had heard a good deal of Prince de Talleyrand from many quarters; but he felt himself bound to declare it to be his sincere and conscientious belief that no man's public and private character had ever been so much belied as the public and private character of that illustrious individual had been. He had thought it necessary, in common justice, to say this much of an individual respecting whose conduct and character he had no small means of forming a judgement.[15]

Few people in Europe were more respected – or better known for their plain speaking – than the Duke of Wellington. When Talleyrand saw the report of the debate in *The Times* next day, he is said to have burst into tears. To Dorothea he confided that this was the first time in his long life that any foreign statesman had ever spoken kindly of him. This was certainly an exaggeration – he was hugely admired in many quarters – but he had been so long accustomed to fending off his detractors that Wellington's words must have given him particular satisfaction. 'In Paris, for which I am killing myself,' he wrote to Princesse de Vaudémont, 'no one would think of saying so much.'[16]

8

'A Firm and Cordial *Entente*'

A LTHOUGH Talleyrand had smartly seen off Flahaut's proposals for dividing Belgium on his visit to London the previous year, he was fond of his son, and as long as he did not trespass on his father's preserves was happy to help him find a post elsewhere. Now 43, Flahaut was an attractive character, gallant, good-looking and eager to please, but lacking in more solid qualities. This became clear when, in June 1831, thanks largely to Talleyrand's influence, he was appointed ambassador in Berlin. The chief aim of his mission – to persuade the Prussians to join with France and Britain in mediating between Russia and Poland – was defeated when both the Prussians and the British refused to intervene. Warsaw fell to the Russians soon later, and after only three months in the post Flahaut decided to return to Paris. Perhaps he was influenced by the fact that an epidemic of cholera, which had broken out in Eastern Europe some months earlier, had now reached Prussia; perhaps he still had his eyes on the embassy in London. 'I am planning to leave Berlin this evening to take advantage of the leave the king has offered me,' he wrote to Talleyrand on 25 September.

> I haven't been feeling at all well for the last few weeks and I also need to be in Paris for my affairs. Will I see you? It seems to me that you above

all deserve to repose yourself, now your task [the withdrawal of French forces from Belgium] is finished.[1]

The hint, if it was one, was delicately made. Meanwhile, in Paris, his wife, a far stronger character, was openly scheming to take over the embassy. It was hard to attack Talleyrand directly, except to emphasise his age and increasing infirmity. She concentrated her efforts on blackening Dorothea's reputation, making much of her former love affairs and hinting at her intrigue with Bacourt. Dorothea knew that Madame de Flahaut was doing her best to undermine her and for that reason alone would have tried to stop Flahaut coming to London. But Talleyrand needed no persuading. 'I have no intention of leaving London,' he wrote to Princesse de Vaudémont.

> This is one of the stories that Madame de Flahaut puts about. She thinks of nothing but returning to England and she cannot return because they cordially dislike her here and because her husband is not a big enough man for London. He would be suitable in other ways for he is affable, knows a great many people and speaks English well. But here that is not enough.[2]

Meanwhile, the work of the conference was continuing. The first task, once the French troops had withdrawn from Belgium, was to impose a six-week armistice on Holland, whose army still stood threateningly near the Belgian frontier. The next was to find a compromise between the *Bases de séparation* agreed with Holland in December 1830 and the Eighteen Articles of the following July. This time there was a general will to find a definitive solution and the conference proceeded far more quickly as a result. The fact that Leopold had needed foreign help to save his kingdom had weakened his position and he was no longer able to demand such favourable terms as before. He ended up with more than the original *Bases de séparation*, including the western part of Luxembourg, but less than the Eighteen Articles; he was also made responsible for nearly half the national debt of the former Kingdom of the Netherlands. The Dutch would recover eastern Luxembourg and its fortress from the Belgians, but were required to evacuate Antwerp, where their troops had been in occupation since the beginning of the dispute. There were to be safeguards on the dykes and sluices – the Dutch had flooded part of Flanders during their attack on Belgium – and navigation of the Scheldt, a key point in British eyes, was to be open to shipping of all nations. By the middle of October, the conference had come to a decision on all main questions, and the two earlier treaties were replaced by the so-called Twenty-Four Articles, a final – and once more 'irrevocable' – treaty to be signed by all five powers.

The Belgian government, indignant at their loss of territory and the amount of debt they had to pay, instructed their ambassador, the young Sylvain Van de Weyer, not to sign the treaty. Palmerston, however, managed to bring him round. He described the process in a private letter, written at three in the morning of 12 November, just after the terms of the treaty had been agreed:

> I have been at Van de Weyer all yesterday and today and have persuaded him the only use of a plenipotentiary is to disobey his instructions and that a clerk or a messenger would do, if it is only necessary strictly to follow them. I have got him, therefore, to throw overboard most of what he was instructed to do... I am writing in the conference, Matusiewicz copying out a note for our signature, old Talley jazzing and telling stories to Lieven and Esterházy and Wessenberg... and the patient Van de Weyer in the adjoining room waiting to know his fate and scratching out and altering just as we tell him to do.[3]

On 15 November, the Twenty-Four Articles were signed by Belgium and all five powers, Leopold having threatened his government to resign if they did not accept them. The Dutch maintained what Palmerston called a

1 Talleyrand at the age of 74 from a portrait by Ary Scheffer. The portrait attracted crowds when it was exhibited in the window of Colnaghi's in 1834.

2 The Duchesse de Dino, Talleyrand's niece by marriage, and his hostess and companion during his embassy in London. The vignette (*c.*1830) is the frontispiece to her memoirs.

3 The Duc d'Orléans takes the oath as Louis-Philippe I, king of the French, in the Chamber of Deputies on 9 August 1830. Lithograph by Lemercier.

4 The July Revolution, 1830: fighting at the rue de Rohan on 29 July, by Hippolyte Lecomte.

5 Adélaïde d'Orléans, Louis-Philippe's sister and closest adviser, by Marie-Amélie Cogniet, 1838.

6 *The Protocol Society in an Uproar, or the Conferees Confounded. A Sketch in Downing Street.* Henry Heath, *c.* August 1831. Talleyrand, seated on the left, smiles at Palmerston, while casually receiving a paper marked 'Private' from a French courier. Other figures include Prince Lieven (standing centre), Baron von Bülow and Prince Esterházy; Leopold and the Prince of Orange hurry off on the right.

7 *The Library at Holland House* by C. R. Leslie, 1838. Lord
Holland is seated on the left, Lady Holland on the right.

8 *A Tête à Tête*: Talleyrand in conversation with Lord Holland
by the political cartoonist HB [John Doyle], 1831.

9 Viscount Palmerston, Whig foreign secretary during Talleyrand's stay in London, after the portrait by Conrad L'Allemand, *c.*1830s–40s.

10 *The Lame Leading the Blind* – cartoon by HB [John Doyle], January 1832. The blind Lord Palmerston is led by the limping Talleyrand.

11 William IV, after the portrait by James Lonsdale, 1830.

12 Leopold I, king of the Belgians by George Dawe. *c.*1830s–40s.

13 Princess Lieven, Russian ambassadress during Talleyrand's stay in London, after John Lucas, *c.*1830s.

14 *La Quadruple Alliance*: French caricature of 1834. Talleyrand, dressed as a bishop, holds an opened Bible. Four crowned monarchs are swearing their oath by placing their hands on the holy book. Left to right: the rotund Louis-Philippe I, the infant Isabella II of Spain, supported by a baby-walker, the girlish Maria II of Spain, carrying a doll, and William IV.

15 *L'apoplexie allant remplacer à Londres la paralysie* (Apoplexy on its way to replace paralysis in London), 26 February 1835. Caricature by Daumier of Talleyrand's replacement by Sébastiani as French ambassador in London.

16 Valençay, a nineteenth-century view of Talleyrand's chateau in Berry, bought at the suggestion of Napoleon in 1803.

sulky silence, but the signatures of the others were sufficient to guarantee the settlement without them. 'The treaty arrived yesterday evening, my dear prince,' wrote Madame Adélaïde to Talleyrand on 18 November.

> I can't tell you the pleasure I got at the sight of the garland of seals from the representatives of five powers, together with our beloved colours. It is a tremendous undertaking that you have just completed and I send you my compliments from the bottom of my heart. For certainly it needed all your zeal, all your talent, all your skill to arrive at this happy conclusion, so important for the happiness of our country, and in truth for all of Europe.[4]

Of course, there were rocks ahead. The treaty had to be ratified by the governments involved; the question of the fortresses was not settled; Holland remained a problem and Dutch troops were still in possession of Antwerp. (The king of Holland, remarked William IV, was 'an obstinate hound.') But the main outlines had been laid down: Belgium was neutral and independent; France was no longer hemmed in by the barrier of the United Netherlands, created as a buffer state at the Congress of Vienna; the threat of European war had been lifted. The greatest triumph had been to bring the three northern powers – Russia, Austria and Prussia – to accept the principle of a constitutional monarchy, when they themselves were committed to autocratic rule. Fear of the spread of revolution had been one of the chief factors, but above all it was the combined strength of France and Britain that had swayed the final settlement. Between them they represented a force too great to be resisted without general war, and with troubles of their own at home, the other powers had no wish to be drawn into one.

Talleyrand's great aim, the alliance of Britain and France, had been achieved. The phrase 'l'entente cordiale', so well known in the following century, was first used by Palmerston in the context of the Belgian treaty – he described it in the Commons as a 'firm and cordial *entente*'[5] – and he had played at least as great a role as Talleyrand in its creation. It was unfortunate, therefore, that not everyone acknowledged it. It was not only Londonderry who thought that Palmerston had allowed himself to be manipulated by the artful Talleyrand. A well-known political cartoonist, 'HB' (John Doyle), made the point in a caricature of Talleyrand and Palmerston entitled *The Lame Leading the Blind*. The likenesses were perfect, the foreign secretary tall and upright, the ambassador limping on his stick, but there was no doubt who was leading whom. HB's cartoons, exhibited monthly in London print shops and sold over the counter for small sums, had none of the savagery of earlier artists, such as Gillray, and most politicians took them in their stride. Palmerston, however, was stung by this particular caricature, and according to Talleyrand never forgave him for it. There was nothing he could do about it, he wrote, but it did not make life easier between them.

Luckily, Talleyrand was on the best of terms with the prime minister, Lord Grey, whose tact and diplomacy often helped to smooth rough corners where Palmerston was concerned. Meeting frequently at Holland House, as well as on official occasions, the two men had learned to appreciate one another's qualities. Just over a year earlier, Grey, in his cups, had been heard to refer to Talleyrand as one of the three greatest rascals in Europe. He had now succumbed completely to the veteran statesman's charm. Writing of Talleyrand to her brother, Count Benckendorff, soon after, Princess Lieven summed up the state of play: 'Grey is devoted to him, Palmerston detests him and Holland tells him all the Cabinet secrets.'[6]

Holland's close relationship with Talleyrand was well known: another cartoon by HB, *A Tête à Tête*, shows the two men deep in conversation, Talleyrand with white hair flowing to his shoulders, Holland with a gouty foot in bandages. A storm in a teacup blew up that December over the long-running saga of the fortresses. Determined to keep France out of it, Palmerston had persuaded the other three powers and Belgium to draw up a secret convention deciding which fortresses should be destroyed;

the French could then be presented with a fait accompli. In submitting the treaty to the Cabinet, however, he failed to warn them not to tell Talleyrand, 'forgetting at the moment,' as he afterwards explained, 'that he is every evening at Holland's elbow'.[7] Talleyrand, who already suspected that something was afoot, managed to worm it out of Holland that very evening.

Holland was unrepentant in the row that followed. 'You miscalculate,' he wrote to Granville in Paris,

> if you imagine that we, that our friends, or what is more material the House of Commons or the Country are prepared to go to war or to spend one sixpence for the demolition of or preservation of all or any of the fortresses in Belgium – still less for preserving to Prussia, Austria and ourselves the right in common with ourselves of dictating what places should remain fortified in a neutral country.[8]

Holland spoke with the voice of reason. The question of the fortresses had been blown out of all proportion. Palmerston had been unnecessarily high-handed in excluding France from the other powers' discussions, but Louis-Philippe and his government were just as ill-advised in turning their destruction into a matter of national prestige. In vain Talleyrand argued that the fortresses were of no importance now that Belgium was a neutral country; Louis-Philippe was determined to make political capital out of their destruction, and refused to ratify the main Belgian treaty, so painfully arrived at by the conference, till a satisfactory solution had been agreed.

Seldom had Talleyrand's patience been so sorely tried. But the king was seeking popularity at home, where, despite the steady hand of Périer, the country was in a discontented mood. Unemployment and bad harvests had led to a series of riots, the most serious of which, an insurrection by silk workers in Lyons, left the city at the mercy of the insurgents for nearly a week. A failed attempt to assassinate the royal family during a ball at the Tuileries soon afterwards drove Talleyrand into a frenzy of anxiety. 'I beseech you to tell me your news,' he wrote to Madame Adélaïde. 'I know nothing; no one has written to me. I beg you not to leave me in total ignorance of something that so nearly affects you.'[9]

It was easy to feel that law and order were breaking down on all sides for the situation in Britain was equally alarming. On 8 October the Reform Bill had been defeated in the House of Lords. The news was greeted by a wave of violence. Angry demonstrations took place across the country; mobs broke the Duke of Wellington's windows; rioters in Bristol set fire to the gaol and town hall; the Duke of Newcastle's house in Nottingham was razed to the ground; Tory MPs went in fear of their lives. Against this threatening background the most important question confronting the country was whether the government would resign. Lady Holland, who adored her position as a great Whig hostess, was appalled at the prospect of her husband losing office: 'Mama's agony at the idea of going out was monstrously diverting, if it were not one's mother,' reported her son, Charles Fox, to his brother.

> 'Your Papa is what I feel about... now really I cannot say how much it vexes me to think of him... If you knew of the little things... the little feeling of doing good... foreign politicks, the great hobby of his Uncle [Fox], of France and England, and still more his own.'
>
> I interrupted and most impudently... said, 'Oh you mean Mama, that he and old Talleyrand are to keep the peace of Europe, don't you?'
>
> My Lady looked angry, and of course was quick enough to say immediately, 'Oh, you may hold your father cheap &c., &c.' However my shot told, which was all I wanted.'[10]

Fortunately for Lady Holland's peace of mind, Grey agreed to stay in office, on condition that the king support the introduction of a new bill, unchanged except for a few small details, in December. Grey's decision to stay, thought Talleyrand, would do much to calm the situation; all the same, he wrote to Princesse de Vaudémont, 'it is a difficult moment, above all for those who have seen what happens when political movements are taken over by the populace.'[11]

In the midst of these anxieties there were moments of light relief, and Lord Holland's diaries give us pleasant glimpses of evenings spent at Holland House. In the entry for 16 January 1832, for instance, he abandons Cabinet matters to describe an exceptionally congenial dinner party at which Melbourne, Sydney Smith and Francis Jeffrey (the editor of the *Edinburgh Review*) were present:

> I scarcely ever heard more wit, learning and good sense in any society, and the remaining part of the Evening did not fall off when Talleyrand came and closed it with some anecdotes, both political and literary, in which his conversation abounds.[12]

On another evening Talleyrand came round to read the first part of his memoirs, 'beautifully written, full of wit and *feeling*'. The aged cynic was unexpectedly shy when he read them:

> They spoke with great taste and delicacy but with deep and natural feeling of the conduct of his parents, and Mother in particular, who neglected and slighted him in his childhood and forced him into the Church when grown up, from an indulgence of their own passions of family pride and wounded vanity on his becoming lame from an accident in infancy. We sat up till three. I could have sat up till sunrise and from thence to sunset to hear these memoirs.[13]

It is a touchingly human glimpse, not only of Talleyrand himself but of the respect and affection with which he was regarded by his friends in Holland House.

9

The Triumph of Reform

T<small>ALLEYRAND</small> had begun his memoirs in 1809, during the four years before the fall of Napoleon when he himself was out of favour; he resumed them during the Restoration and would complete them after leaving London in 1834. Not always wholly reliable, and at times 'improved' by Bacourt, their lucidity and intelligence reveal him as one of the masters of French prose; even Sainte-Beuve, who detested him, praised the clarity and correctness of his style. They deal with politics, rather than his private life, and apart from the early chapters, which refer so movingly to his unhappy childhood, their tone is generally impersonal. What is surprising is that two and a half of the five volumes are devoted to Talleyrand's time in London: the events of the Revolution, the Directory, the Napoleonic era and the Congress of Vienna are dealt with in far less detail than the long negotiations over Belgium. Despite moments of inconsistency, hesitation and sometimes sheer frustration, they were, he considered, his finest work.

The text for this London period consists largely of official documents – protocols, diplomatic despatches, notes to Palmerston and Grey – linked by explanatory passages. It is also enlivened by Talleyrand's letters to Princesse de Vaudémont (returned to him after her death), by his informal exchanges with Madame Adélaïde and – not yet mentioned in these pages – by the occasional letters of his friend the Duc de Dalberg.

Of German origin but French by nationality, the duke had served under Talleyrand as a member of the provisional government in 1814 and as one of his ministers at the Congress of Vienna. Worldly and sardonic, he had now retired from public life, but continued to cast a knowledgeable eye on the European scene. Here he is, for instance, referring to Louis-Philippe's first ministry – 'democratic anarchy'; to the madness of Lord Londonderry – 'he's never been any different'; or to Flahaut's stint as ambassador in Prussia – 'he cuts a poor kind of figure in Berlin'. And when, at the end of December 1831, the foreign minister, Sébastiani, suffered a stroke which left him semi-paralysed, his reaction was typically irreverent: *'Your chief'* – the emphasis was sarcastic – 'Sébastiani, owes his indisposition to his buffoon-like behaviour while addressing the tribune in the Luxembourg [palace]. He puffed himself out like a toad to make his effect and the blood rushed to his head.'[1] Talleyrand usually enjoyed his friend's dismissive comments, but with so much still to be decided over Belgium, the news of Sébastiani's illness was a serious blow. 'I'm truly upset by Sébastiani's accident,' he wrote to Princesse de Vaudémont.

> He had his drawbacks, but he also had his virtues. He had skill and *savoir vivre*, and I'm sure was well disposed; all that counts for something... At present we need to finish the Belgian affair – we'll get there whatever any one says. I may die in the attempt like Sébastiani; but it is my chosen field of battle. Please God it will be a field of honour.[2]

At the end of December, without consulting Talleyrand, the other powers signed their agreement on the fortresses: all but three of them – many of them already in ruins – were to be demolished. There was great indignation in Paris that the deal had been done behind France's back, and that two of the fortresses to be destroyed – Marienberg and Philippeville – had actually belonged to France. Talleyrand knew there was nothing further to be done; heavily influenced by Palmerston, the other powers were never going to change their minds. In any case, he told Princesse de Vaudémont, once the principle of demolition was accepted they ceased to be important:

> It's only a stupid question of *amour propre* that's involved. If there isn't a war they [the fortresses] will fall down because no one will repair them; if there is a war we'll take them back. That's all there is to it.[3]

Talleyrand's plain speaking, filtered through to the king and Périer, had its effect. The French government was forced to swallow its pride; it was not worth going to war for two fortresses. On the evening of 31 January 1832, Britain, France and Belgium finally ratified the treaty of 15 November, guaranteeing Belgium's frontiers and its status as a neutral state. The governments of Austria, Russia and Prussia had yet to do the same, but Talleyrand was confident that they would follow. 'That done,' he wrote to Princesse de Vaudémont, 'we'll have to wait for the Dutch and no one much cares what they say. Spain once spent 24 years in a similar situation, and Europe wasn't inconvenienced.'[4] The evacuation of Dutch troops from Antwerp was another matter, but he hoped that time and persuasion would gradually have their effect.

What had become of the famous principle of non-intervention, the conference's watchword at the outset of its meetings? 'Non-intervention,' Palmerston now declared in the Commons, 'is not an English word,'[5] while Talleyrand, when asked its meaning by the Whig peer Lord Alvanley, made a wittily evasive answer: 'Non-intervention,' he explained, 'is a metaphysical and political term which means more or less the same as intervention.'[6] But the term had served its purpose at the time of the Belgian revolution and could still be invoked on future occasions.

Talleyrand had always prided himself on his good relations with Périer, who had sent his son to work under him as a junior attaché in London, and who had usually agreed with him on most foreign issues. In February 1832, however, following a new uprising in the Papal States the Austrians sent in troops to back the government and Périer, under pressure from liberal opinion, sent a small force to the rebel city of Ancona in response. Talleyrand was furious. Two or three thousand men in Ancona could do nothing for the liberal cause; the Austrians had an army of 70,000 men committed to upholding the pope's reactionary regime. All it could do was to create bad blood between the French and Austrians and provide an excuse for holding up the ratification of the Belgian treaty; Russia and Prussia would then follow suit. The whole expedition, he wrote to Princesse de Vaudémont, was utter madness: 'I'm not going to give up, but this affair is killing me.'[7]

He expressed himself more soberly in his memoirs:

I thought that the [government] was plunging itself precipitately into new difficulties, without having resolved those which had held peace in suspense for the last 18 months... I was not unaware that in Paris the opposition was protesting loudly against the entry of the Austrian troops into the papal territories but I thought that with a little more firmness one could have resisted their cries until the treaty of 15 November 1831 was ratified by all the powers... I am certain that we would then have gained the agreement of the English government to take action based on treaties and the principle of non-intervention, judiciously applied.[8]

In the long run no lasting harm was done. Neither Périer nor Louis-Philippe had any desire to go to war with Austria, and having made their gesture to liberal opinion were happy to find a face-saving way out. In this they were helped by Palmerston, who sent an unofficial emissary (Britain had no diplomatic relations with Rome) to work with the French and Austrian ministers to settle the difficulties between the pope and his subjects. Some concessions were promised (though never carried out) and the pope agreed to the French presence in Ancona until the Austrian troops had left the Papal States.

All this would take some time to achieve. The immediate result in London was to fuel Tory suspicions of France's revolutionary sympathies – particularly unfortunate for the Whigs at a time when their opponents were already prophesying civil war and revolution if the Reform Bill went through. Talleyrand did his best to play things down, much helped by his good relationship with Grey. When Aberdeen, speaking for the Tories, attacked the French occupation of Ancona in the House of Lords as 'worse than any of the Republick or Napoleon', Grey was able to deflect his ire.[9] Explanations had been required, he explained, and there was every reason to believe that that they would be satisfactory; he was certain that the French government had no sinister intentions. This seemed to be the general opinion. 'The Ancona affair will blow over,' wrote Greville in his diary. 'It was a little escapade of Périer's, done in a hurry, a mistake... Talleyrand told me "c'est une bêtise".'[10]

It was a tribute to Talleyrand's standing that the Ancona affair caused so little trouble. In London his reputation as a statesman was at its height: he was respected and admired by politicians of both parties; his presence conferred distinction on the grandest gatherings; his bons mots, as one diarist put it, flew round the drawing rooms of London. (He himself declared that he had never uttered a bon mot in his life; 'but I endeavour,' he once said, 'after much reflection, on many subjects, to find the *mot juste*.'[11]) Professional gossips, like Creevey, who did not speak French, bewailed what they were missing: 'What an idiot I am,' he wrote, 'never to have made myself a Frenchman. To think of having such a card as this old villain Talleyrand so often within one's reach and yet not to be able to make anything of it.'[12]

Dorothea was equally admired in her own sphere, as much for her cleverness – Talleyrand told Greville she was the cleverest person, male or female, he had ever met – as for her charm and beauty. After 18 months in London she had come to appreciate the special qualities of the English: the women, whose fine figures and fresh complexions redeemed their lack of expression and taste in clothes; the men, cold and reserved at first sight, but concealing a wealth of learning and good sense behind their apparent shyness. As well as enjoying the social round in London, she and Talleyrand were invited to some of England's grandest country houses, Dorothea taking a particular interest in their history, architecture and works of art. At Warwick Castle she met with the country-house convention – unthinkable in France – of banishing the ladies to the drawing room while the men lingered over their port after dinner and gave an amusing description of the evening in her journal:

> On leaving the table, a very long time before the men, we were conducted
> to the great salon... I have never in my life known anything so sad and
> *chilling* [she uses the English word] as this salon; women's conversation,
> very languishing... it seemed as though the portrait of Charles I and the
> Black Prince were joining in, and taking their coffee by the fire... I was
> reminded a thousand times of the description Corinne gives of staying
> with her mother in law.[13]

(In Madame de Staël's novel *Corinne*, the French heroine suffers similar banishment with the ladies while staying with her English husband's family in the north of England.)

It was a relief to return from such scenes to the 'smoke and politics' of London, which in the spring of 1832 was in a state of feverish excitement. The Reform Bill overshadowed all other subjects of conversation. 'The bill, the whole bill, and nothing but the bill' was the slogan with which the measure had been presented; a second rejection by the House of Lords, in most people's opinion, would lead to civil war. Meanwhile the cholera epidemic which had been sweeping Eastern Europe had reached Britain, moving southwards from Scotland at the beginning of the year. In London the epidemic was largely confined to the docks and the East End. On 29 March, however, cholera broke out in Paris and spread through the whole city with terrifying speed. On 3 April, after a courageous visit to the cholera wards in the central Paris hospital, the Hôtel-Dieu, the prime minister, Périer, succumbed to the disease.

Events were moving so fast that even the long-awaited ratifications of the Belgian treaty by Russia, Austria and Prussia seemed something of an anticlimax. Would Périer survive – and if not who would succeed him? Would the Lords accept the Reform Bill – and if not would there be a civil war? The first question was already being mooted within days of Périer falling ill. For many, including Madame Adélaïde, Talleyrand was the obvious replacement for Périer or, should he recover, for Sébastiani, whose health was still uncertain after his stroke. Talleyrand, however, had no intention of accepting either post. To his old friend, the finance minister Baron Louis, who had been asked to approach him unofficially, he explained his reasons for refusing:

Here's my opinion: one should devote oneself to what one knows, and never take on something unless one's sure of doing it better than anyone else. That's why I wanted you to be finance minister; no one could do it better than you; and that's why I came to London, in the belief that no one else was so well qualified to keep the peace... At present, I'll stay on here till the aim of my journey has been accomplished, or is on the point of being so. After that I'll ask for four months' leave to take the waters and to look after my affairs, of which I've seen nothing for the last two years; ever since I've been in London I haven't given a moment's thought to anything not leading to the result we need so much, for without peace who knows what will happen to us all?[14]

The end was now in sight, with the ratification of the Belgian treaty safely in hand. But there was too much happening in London for him to leave immediately. On 14 April, the second reading of the Reform Bill in the House of Lords went through with a majority of nine. The Tories were still determined to block it. Their aim was to nibble away at the bill by a series of amendments which would change its essential character while avoiding a major confrontation. Grey saw the trap they were preparing. When the government was defeated by the Tories on a seemingly unimportant point of procedure he seized his opportunity; either the king would make sufficient peers to enable him to pass the bill in its entirety, or he would resign.

The king, who hoped that the Tories would be able to pass a more moderate version of the bill without the creation of new peers, accepted Grey's resignation. On 9 May he turned to Wellington to form an administration. During the nine days that followed, 'the days of May' as they were called, Britain held its breath. Perhaps never, since the seventeenth century, had the country been closer to civil war. Instead of the spontaneous outbreaks of the previous year, there was a feeling of silent but determined resistance, of violence barely held in check. Mass meetings were held across the country; in London the radical leader Francis Place campaigned for a run on the banks – 'To stop the duke, go for gold.' 'Extraordinary times!' wrote Talleyrand to Princesse de Vaudémont.[15] Never had it been more important for France to appear stable and free of revolutionary influences. It was her turn to set a good example to her neighbour.

Wellington had agreed to form a government out of loyalty to the king, but it soon became clear that the Tory party was not prepared to follow him, and after a series of fruitless negotiations he abandoned the attempt. The ball was now in Grey's court, and since he refused to take office unless new peers were created the king was forced to give in. 'Grey's ministry stays,' wrote Talleyrand dramatically to Princesse de Vaudémont on 16 May; 'the details are being arranged as I write.'[16] Britain had drawn back from the brink of revolution; the same day, however, brought devastating news from Paris. After six weeks hovering between life and death, Périer had died that morning.

'Poor Talleyrand is cruelly cut up by the death of Périer,' wrote Lady Holland.[17] Nor was he tempted by renewed suggestions that he should take Périer's place. The Comte de Rémusat, son of an old friend of

Talleyrand, and a leading member of the Doctrinaires, a right-wing party, was sent to London to sound him out. He found the ambassador much aged, he wrote in his memoirs: his features were flaccid and drooping; his face was creased with new wrinkles, but he was as lively in spirit and intelligence as ever. He questioned Rémusat closely on what was happening in France. There was only one point on which he fell silent and let the conversation drop: it was that of leading the new government. 'I saw straight away,' wrote Rémusat,

> that he had no desire to do so; but that it cost him a little to say so, not wishing to give reasons which might sound like an admission that he lacked the strength or ability to take it on.

If he had any doubts in this regard they were quickly dispelled when two or three evenings after his arrival Dorothea invited him to lunch next day. The lunch took place in her sitting room, with no servants present, and Rémusat confessed to wondering whether, as he'd heard sometimes happened in high society, she expected him to make a love scene of it: 'Happily neither the temptation nor my self-esteem so far blinded me; I saved myself from ridicule and contented myself by eating my eggs and cutlets and trying to keep my wits about me.'

They discussed many subjects over lunch, but the main object of the conversation was to tell him the following:

> You want to make Monsieur de Talleyrand into a head of Government? Spare yourself the trouble of trying; it would not suit him at all. He does not wish to do it, and even if he did, I would not permit it.

'At these words, or something like them,' wrote Rémusat, 'I said, "That's enough, Madame. I know when I'm beaten."'[18]

Thereafter, in talking to Talleyrand, Rémusat was just sufficiently insistent to make it appear that he was not giving up too easily before accepting his refusal. Dorothea had been right; Talleyrand, who could now hardly walk, was no longer in a state to plunge into the turbulence and passions of French politics. In London he was doing what no one else could so well and though the task would not be completed till the Dutch had been brought into line, enough had been achieved for him to take a few months' leave. The Reform Bill had gone through the Lords on 23 May, sufficient Tory peers abstaining to make the creation of new peers unnecessary; it would pass into law two weeks later. A deputy ambassador whom Talleyrand approved of had been found; William IV and Palmerston had been informed of his intentions; the time had now come, as he told Princesse de Vaudémont, to think of his eyes, his legs and his own affairs.

10

Leave of Absence

{ ——— }

T ALLEYRAND planned to leave London at the end of June. His deputy ambassador, Baron Durand de Mareuil, was an experienced career diplomat who could be relied on to follow the line laid down by Talleyrand: 'Union with England, good relations with the five powers, general agreement on making the king of Holland give back Belgian territory and above all evacuating Antwerp.'[1]

The only person who was unhappy with the arrangement was Flahaut. With his well-connected wife and many friends among the Whigs, he had expected to be given the post himself – it would have been a natural step towards succeeding his father when he retired. He had always had a high opinion of his own abilities – he would later complain to his wife that Louis-Philippe would have made him foreign minister but for Talleyrand's opposition. Now he wrote dejectedly to Talleyrand's old crony Montrond complaining that Talleyrand had not even considered him before choosing Mareuil. Montrond had his own ideas why this was so. 'You ask why they have not sent for you,' he wrote. 'There are some things that I hardly dare to admit to you, much less write, so you will have to wait till I see you.'[2]

Montrond was probably referring to Dorothea's hidden influence: she would almost certainly have done her best to block Flahaut's appointment. Flahaut had long detested Dorothea – he described her privately as a 'horrid little serpent'[3] – but he had always tried to please his father, and had, as he thought, behaved with the utmost tact and consideration on his visits to London the previous year. Hurt feelings turned to resentment. From now on relations between the two men worsened, Flahaut's sense of grievance fuelled by his wife, Talleyrand increasingly irritated by the couple's intrigues. 'His animosity against [Flahaut],' wrote a friend the following year, 'is now as lively as his affection for him used to be.'[4]

'Everyone at the conference is in a great hurry to finish things before M. de Talleyrand leaves,' Montrond had told Flahaut.[5] But any chance of a peaceful run-up to his departure was thrown into confusion by two violent uprisings in France. The first took place in the traditionally royalist area of the Vendée, where the Duchesse de Berry, having landed in Marseilles the previous month, had raised an army of supporters for her son. On 6 June they were roundly defeated by government troops. The duchess fled, a few arrests were made and the episode ended in farce a few months later when the duchess, on being captured and imprisoned, was discovered to be pregnant. She was obliged to reveal her secret marriage to an Italian count and, considered discredited by this *mésalliance*, was released soon afterwards.

Talleyrand, according to Lord Holland, had not been alarmed by this first upheaval, though he lamented the bloodshed and useless sacrifices involved. Far more serious was the republican insurrection which took place in Paris at almost the same time. The occasion was the funeral of the liberal general Lamarque, a victim of cholera, on 5 June. Attended by huge crowds of left-wing sympathisers, the funeral procession soon turned into rebellion. The two days that followed are immortalised in Victor Hugo's *Les Misérables*, and in this way, in the words of one historian, 'have provided probably the definitive image of nineteenth-century Parisian revolution, with its banners, barricades and furious battles between government troops and shirtsleeved workers.'[6]

The insurrection was on the scale of the July Revolution, but the response was very different. The government troops were well prepared;

Louis-Philippe, on horseback, displayed exemplary skill and courage in directing their movements and rallying popular support. After two days of furious street fighting and the loss of 800 lives, the insurgents were defeated. Seven of the ringleaders were condemned to death, though their sentences were later commuted to life imprisonment. The British, when dealing with their own disturbances, were less humane. After a peaceful demonstration by starving agricultural labourers the previous year, three men had been hanged and 57 transported.

Talleyrand had seen too much of mob violence to be anything but appalled by the news of the uprising. Lack of information made his worries even worse. 'The courier has just arrived,' he wrote to Princesse de Vaudémont on 7 June, 'and I have no letters from you today, at a time when the whole town is full of deplorable news from Paris. I am horribly uneasy.'[7]

Writing to her the following morning, he was no better informed:

I'm starting this letter before having news from Paris. I've heard nothing since the 6th, at nine in the morning; judge of my torment. I hope that things turn out to the advantage of the government, and that the government will profit from them to re-establish good order, so gravely shaken at the moment, by strong and constitutional means. It is in order, constitutionally established, that one should seek popularity... Caresses given to the mob [*canaille*] embolden them and produce no other effect.[8]

In fact the June Rising, as it was called, was the last major protest against the July Monarchy. The republicans had been crushed, the royalists discredited; the death of Napoleon's son, the Duc de Reichstadt, at Schönbrunn that summer would remove the immediate hopes of the Bonapartist party. To a public tired of violence and uncertainty Louis-Philippe, though he satisfied few of the revolution's deeper aspirations, offered the best hope of stability. Delacroix's famous painting *Liberty*

Leading the People had symbolised the spirit of 1830. Its fate was equally symbolic: exhibited in 1831 and bought by the state as a sop to popular opinion, it was withdrawn from public view after June 1832. It would not reappear until 1848.

With two insurrections safely behind him, the last few weeks of Talleyrand's stay in London passed peacefully. There was an end-of-term feeling about them. Grey gave a farewell dinner; his relations with his fellow ambassadors had never been better; even Palmerston was unexpectedly gracious. 'Goodbye again, my dear prince,' he wrote on the eve of his departure; 'give good advice where you are going, take good care of yourself, recover your health quickly after the long fatigues of our conferences, and come back soon, but above all come back.'[9]

Talleyrand's final call was at Holland House. 'Prince Talleyrand took leave of us this night,' wrote Holland in his journal for 19 June.

> He was manifestly affected at leaving England and though earnest in his assurance of returning seemed to me to have misgivings that he should not... Our King, who was strongly prejudiced against Talleyrand on his arrival in England, complimented him in his audience of leave extremely on his conduct, attributed to his talents and good disposition the understanding subsisting between the two countries, vehemently expressed the hope that he might return and directed Palmerston in his presence to write to Paris to assure Louis-Philippe that nothing could be more pleasing to the Govt. here or more calculated to prove his earnest desire of peace between two countries, than his return.[10]

It would have been hard to leave under more favourable circumstances. Did the contrast with his humiliating departure during the French Revolution strike him? The ideas he had taken with him then – a constitutional monarchy in France, an alliance with Britain – had seemed utterly impossible. Now they had become realities and he had the satisfaction of knowing he had played a major role in achieving both.

Back in France, after a short stay in Paris, Dorothea and Talleyrand parted company, Dorothea for a cure in Switzerland, Talleyrand to take the waters at Bourbon-l'Archambault, well known for helping those with rheumatism. Here, he wrote to the Duc de Broglie, he intended to 'go to bed early, to eat only what is necessary, and not be obliged to say anything of the slightest interest.'[11] But he had hardly settled down to this routine when urgent messages arrived from London, insisting he return at once: 'A new intrigue was brewing. A case was being made that my replacement in London, M. Durand de Mareuil, was not acceptable because I had preferred him to Flahaut, who was General Sébastiani's choice.'[12]

Flahaut, it was true, was a good friend of Sébastiani's, but neither he nor the foreign minister had a chance against the wily Talleyrand. The ambassador had made up his mind not to return to England till October, but he now let it be known that he would be leaving France in August – too soon to make a change worthwhile. 'That put an end to the Flahaut–Sébastiani plot,' he wrote complacently, 'and after that they left me in peace.'[13]

Talleyrand's stay at Bourbon-l'Archambault did nothing for his health: he had a bad fall in his room and ended up with a violent cold. But he found the rest and refreshment he needed at Rochecotte, Dorothea's chateau in Touraine, where they joined up after their respective cures. His niece's house had always been a second home. 'I'm enjoying myself very much,' he wrote to Bacourt, who had stayed behind in London;

> the life we're leading first of all; the air we're breathing; politics at a safe distance, everything delights me. Madame de Dino is quite well; she's recovering; as for me I think I'm picking up strength and I'm sleeping better.[14]

But there was a limit to the charms of rural life. Even from Rochecotte, despite his protestations, Talleyrand was keeping an eye on what was happening in Paris. On 11 October 1832, after several months of uncertainty following Périer's death, a new ministry had been formed under the distinguished Napoleonic marshal, Soult. Sébastiani was replaced by the Duc de Broglie; Thiers, Talleyrand's former protégé, was minister of the interior. (When Montrond, amazed at Thiers's rapid rise to power, described him as a parvenu, Talleyrand quietly put him right: '*Thiers n'est pas un parvenu, il est arrivé*' – Thiers is not a parvenu; he has arrived.[15]) Confident that France now had a stable government, Talleyrand was ready to set out for London once more. 'It seems that the winter will have to be spent in tranquillising Europe,' he wrote to Holland before leaving; 'it's what you and I both want and we must work to achieve this great result.'[16]

He arrived in England after a stormy crossing and almost immediately plunged into a new round of negotiations over Belgium. The continuing refusal of the king of Holland to evacuate his troops from Antwerp had finally compelled the conference to make a stand. Unless the situation was soon resolved, Leopold might take the law into his own hands; Holland would respond; other countries would take sides and the outcome might be a general war. On 1 October the five powers had signed a joint protocol declaring 'that it had become necessary to take coercive measures against Holland to oblige her to execute the conditions of the treaty signed by the five powers and Belgium.'[17] (Holland, of course, had never agreed to this treaty.)

So much was settled by the time Talleyrand arrived in London but the conference was divided sharply about the methods of coercing Holland. The three northern powers, Russia, Austria and Prussia, were only prepared to exert financial pressure; Britain and France, on the other hand, reserved the right to take more effective measures, that is, to use force if necessary. It was in order to see this last negotiation through, wrote Talleyrand, that he had decided to come back to London.

Talleyrand had always got on well with the ambassadors of the northern powers; they shared his desire to keep the peace in Europe, and at various times had managed to restrain their respective foreign secretaries

– Metternich for Austria, Nesselrode for Russia and Humboldt for Prussia – from over-reacting. But there was still a danger of war if Britain and France acted unilaterally. The great thing would be to expel the Dutch troops from Antwerp so quickly that the other powers would have no time to muster their forces. The French, if they undertook the task, would then withdraw immediately; Belgium, meanwhile, would give back those areas of Holland which they were still occupying, and the terms of the treaty of the previous November – the Twenty-Four Articles – would finally be carried out.

For the new French ministry, eager for popular approval, it was important that the question of Antwerp be resolved quickly; the credibility of the government depended on it. The British, on the other hand, had no certainty that Soult's ministry would survive; the last thing they wanted was to find they were acting with a disunited or revolutionary regime. Talleyrand was under pressure from both sides, the French insistent that the matter be dealt with as soon as possible, the British reluctant to move before they had the agreement of all the Cabinet. Nonetheless, on 22 October – 'only eight days after my arrival', wrote Talleyrand – the two powers signed a secret convention agreeing to take joint action against Holland: a combined naval blockade of the coast by France and Britain and an attack by the French army on the Dutch garrison in Antwerp. The convention was ratified in Paris on 25 October, and was kept so secret that Louis-Philippe did not even mention it to Madame Adélaïde. Talleyrand, however, had tipped her off privately. 'I went in to see him triumphantly carrying your precious letter,' she wrote, 'and he burst out laughing, saying "it wasn't me that told you"... Needless to say, there will be no indiscretion on my part.'[18]

As soon as the convention had been ratified in Paris and London the Dutch and Belgian governments were informed that unless they agreed to carry out the terms of the Twenty-Four Articles by 2 November and to put them into practice by 12 November, they would be imposed by force; in the case of a refusal by the Dutch an embargo would be placed on their shipping and on 15 November French troops would enter Belgium in order to besiege Antwerp. The three northern powers were informed at the same time. Russia and Prussia made disapproving noises, but neither they nor Austria were prepared to take active steps to prevent the combined action of France and Britain, and perhaps were even relieved that the matter was out of their hands.

Talleyrand could ascribe much of the success of the agreement first to the good work put in by Mareuil during his absence, and second to the good relations he had built up with Grey and Palmerston. He was deeply irritated, therefore, by the behaviour of Madame de Flahaut. A peeress in her own right (Lady Keith) and a patroness of Almack's, London's most exclusive assembly rooms, she had recently arrived in England and was doing her best to cast doubt on the new ministry. 'Here I am in the midst of Madame de Flahaut's continual intrigues,' he complained to Princesse de Vaudémont.

> She spends her time with Lady Grey, to whom she repeats the worst possible things about our present government – 'It can't last; the ministry won't hold; they won't keep their majority...' That's what she's been saying everywhere. Today she did it at Lord Holland's. To have to conduct difficult negotiations and to put up with this constant social sniping as well is too much. The fact is that her husband in Paris and she in London are doing serious harm to our new ministry, it's truly shameful. I could not believe it when people told me what this ménage was up to; but now I realise I was a great fool to discount the rumours as mere calumnies.[19]

One of the disadvantages of operating as an ambassador in the aristocratic circles in which political power still resided was the damage that could be done in London drawing rooms. In this case Princess Lieven added to Talleyrand's troubles by putting it about that Palmerston (who was one of her former admirers) was at odds with the rest of the Cabinet about joining forces with the French, and that the king, whose loathing of France was well known, would never allow it. Fortunately, neither she nor Madame de Flahaut was as well informed as they thought. The new French ministry showed no signs of falling; the British Cabinet was unanimous in its decision to combine with the French in expelling the Dutch from Antwerp; the king reluctantly agreed – although, as Lord Holland noted, 'he foreboded misfortune from any joint operations with France!'[20] At the beginning of November, in line with their declared intentions, the French and British forces were ready to take action.

11

Besieging Antwerp

W<small>HY</small> had the king of Holland refused to come to terms over Antwerp? Even though his brief invasion of Belgium had brought about the scrapping of the Eighteen Articles, he resented the subsequent Belgian treaty of 15 November 1831, above all the loss of half of Luxembourg, of which he was the hereditary crown prince. With dynastic links to two of the three northern powers (his wife was the sister of the king of Prussia; his son was married to the daughter of the tsar), he still hoped that they would come to his aid if Antwerp – his chief bargaining card – was attacked.

In London Talleyrand waited anxiously for news of the impending action. 'Let me recommend you to do too much rather than enough,' he wrote to Broglie; 'remember that you must have a success.'[1] On 15 November, while the joint fleets of France and Britain blockaded the mouth of the Scheldt, a French army of 60,000 men marched on Antwerp. Their progress was delayed by appalling weather conditions, but on 30 December, after a three-week siege, in which Louis-Philippe's sons fought bravely, the Dutch garrison capitulated. The blockade continued a little longer, to the great detriment of Dutch trade, but by May the following year the Dutch king was forced to make overtures for peace. His behaviour meanwhile had been far from admirable. Expecting a general war over the French invasion, he had engaged in a secret speculation with the financier Gabriel Ouvrard to buy up large quantities of grain, whose price he thought would be bound to rise. In his classic study, *The Foreign Policy of Palmerston*, the historian Sir Charles Webster suggests that Talleyrand too had been involved: 'What speculations that dubious character [Ouvrard]... carried on with Talleyrand and others will no doubt be buried for all time.'[2]

The charge against Talleyrand is unproven, but even Palmerston, with his low opinion of foreigners, was amazed when he heard of the king of Holland's behaviour: 'I cannot conceive,' he wrote to the British attaché in The Hague,

> how a Sovereign, who is in the act of losing half his dominions and who is negotiating with all Europe for the terms of separation, can sit down to turn the corn factor and speculate upon the profit he is to make by selling biscuits to the armies who might make his dominions the area of conflict. *This is very Dutch.*[3]

Talleyrand's memoirs, naturally, make no mention of such matters. The siege of Antwerp had inflicted little damage on the citadel; the Dutch prisoners of war had been freely released; above all – to the immense relief of Talleyrand – his government had kept its word by promptly withdrawing its troops from Belgium. This act of good faith, confirming France's position as a reliable player on the European scene, completed the process of her acceptance by the autocratic powers, as well as consolidating the Anglo-French alliance. It was the goal towards which Talleyrand had been working for the last two years.

Just at this moment of general satisfaction, he had news of the sudden death of Princesse de Vaudémont – her illness had been so swift that she died almost before he heard of it. It was one of Talleyrand's virtues that, with a few exceptions, he always remained on good terms with his former loves. The princess had been part of his youth, and perhaps his closest confidante over the years; latterly, thanks to her intimacy with

Madame Adélaïde, she had been an invaluable link with Louis-Philippe. Clever, liberal-minded, devoted to her friends and the menagerie of pets – dogs, monkeys, parrots – with which she was surrounded, she was, wrote Talleyrand in one of his last letters to her, his 'other self'. It was the loss not only of a friend, but of a way of life. 'In the old days,' he wrote, 'a celebrated salon, a personage of wit and influence could be replaced. Now one sees clearly what has been lost... It is society itself that is ending.'[4] He wept at the news of her death; it was the only time, remarked Montrond, that he had ever seen him cry.

Despite his sorrow at the loss of his old friend, Talleyrand continued to show an imperturbable face to the world. A passionate gambler, he found consolation at the card tables of the Travellers Club, where, according to one member, he 'steered his way as triumphantly through all the mazes of whist and écarté, as he had done amid the intricacies of the thirteen different forms of government... he had sworn to observe.'[5] For Talleyrand, cards were the perfect form of relaxation: 'they are an occupation without being a preoccupation,' he once remarked, 'and save one from making conversation.'[6] His taciturnity at the table, it was said, was wholly British.

The writer Prosper Mérimée, 29 years old, and already one of the leaders of the French Romantic movement, spent the winter of 1832–3 in London. Thanks to an introduction to the ambassador – always ready to welcome rising talent – he had ample opportunities of observing Talleyrand in his English setting. He found his appearance disconcerting: 'a big packet of flannel, enveloped in a blue coat, and surmounted by a death's head covered in parchment.'[7] But he was amazed at the position he held in London society:

> I cannot sufficiently admire the profound good sense of everything he says, the simplicity and *comme il faut* of his manners. It is the perfection of an aristocrat. The English, who have great pretensions to elegance and good taste, come nowhere near him. Wherever he goes he creates

a court and sets the tone. There is nothing more amusing than to see him surrounded by the most influential members of the House of Lords, obsequious and almost servile.

All the same, he added, the prince had a curious habit:

> After dinner, instead of rinsing out his mouth, as is the custom in London and Paris, he rinses out his nose, and here is how he does it. Someone puts a kind of oilcloth napkin under his chin, and he sniffs two glasses of water up his nose, which he then ejects from his mouth. This operation, which does not take place without a considerable noise, occurs at a little buffet at two paces from the table. Thus yesterday, during this singular ablution, all the diplomatic corps, with eyes lowered, stood silently awaiting the end of the operation, and behind the prince, Lady Jersey, napkin in hand, followed the course of the glasses of water with respectful interest; if she had dared, she would have carried the little basin. This Lady Jersey is the haughtiest and most impertinent woman in England; she is very beautiful, witty, cultivated and belongs to the highest nobility. The prince must be a great seducer to inspire such condescension on her part. '*C'est une bien bonne habitude* [a very good habit], *mon prince*', observed the lady. – 'Oh, *très sale, très sale* [very dirty, very dirty]', he replied, and took her arm, having kept her waiting for five minutes.[8]

The one person who did not share the general adoration of Talleyrand was Palmerston. They had worked together well in the months leading up to the treaty of November 1831, and his goodbye wishes for his return to London after his leave had been genuine. But he had found Talleyrand's deputy, Mareuil, far easier to deal with, and, with the appointment of Broglie as foreign minister in France, began communicating with him directly, bypassing Talleyrand in the process. When Molé had tried to do this Wellington had simply passed his letters on to Talleyrand; Palmerston did no such thing. The Antwerp expedition had been a success, and he valued the Anglo-French connection, but he was beginning to feel that 'old Talley' had served his time. His rudeness became noticeable. Once he kept Talleyrand waiting so long outside his door that Grey, embarrassed by his behaviour, came to sit with him himself. In Palmerston's defence, Talleyrand showed scant regard for the foreign secretary's convenience. 'I have never kept him when I could help it,' Palmerston told Granville.

> Other diplomats who want me come and pop into my room... at 12 and come in and go out in a short time; he does not weigh anchor till after one or near two; and what he likes to do is to come and establish himself in the armchair at the office about four, just as I want to go away and eat something before I go down to the House of Commons. This I always fight off; for his visit never lasts less than an hour and that throws us out as to everything to be done afterwards.[9]

In Paris, the new foreign minister, the Duc de Broglie, was proving less biddable than Talleyrand's old disciple Sébastiani. He hugely admired Talleyrand, and recognised his value to the July Monarchy as Europe's most distinguished statesman. But this did not mean that he was prepared to hand over the direction of foreign policy to him, or indeed to Louis-Philippe, who had briefly taken over as foreign minister in the interim after Périer's death. He was happy to go along with Palmerston's policy of dealing with him direct, rather than through the embassy in London, and though Talleyrand complained to Louis-Philippe from time to time the new ministry was not yet established enough for the king to risk annoying Broglie. And Talleyrand, after all, was now nearly 80 and could not be expected to last forever.

Talleyrand chafed at these constraints, though thanks to his wide range of contacts he usually found ways of getting round them. He was still determined to see the Belgian question through, in the teeth of the king of Holland, who, faithful to his system of ruse and procrastination, was doing everything in his power to avoid recognising the treaty of 15 November and to maintain a provisional state of affairs which left him free to go to war again if conditions should prove favourable.[10]

It is possible to understand his exasperation, but it is hard not to feel some sympathy for the Dutch, who had signed the original Eighteen Articles in good faith, only to have them rewritten under pressure from Leopold less than a year later.

On 29 January 1833, the reformed House of Commons met for the first time. 'I never saw so many shocking bad hats in my life,' remarked the Duke of Wellington as he surveyed the new intake. The election had been an overwhelming victory for the Whigs, but its immediate result was to distract the government's attention from foreign affairs. 'One mustn't lose sight of the fact that home affairs here take precedence over all others, however important they may be,' wrote Talleyrand to Broglie on 31 January. 'Parliament has only just assembled; the Cabinet has to deal with the questions which preoccupy them most: the state of Ireland, tithes for the clergy, financial problems... and it is almost impossible to divert them from such pressing matters.'[11]

Quite apart from Belgium, there were major foreign issues to consider, in each case demanding the joint attention of Britain and France. On the Iberian peninsula, a civil war in Portugal was raging between the former emperor of Brazil, Dom Pedro, battling for the rights of his 14-year-old daughter, Dona Maria, against his usurping brother Dom Miguel, the de facto ruler of the country. Since Miguel was a ferocious reactionary, and Pedro and his daughter were mildly liberal, French and British sympathies were with the latter, though neither country was prepared to enter into full-scale conflict on their behalf. Meanwhile, in Spain, where the current monarch, Ferdinand VII, was gravely ill, a potential conflict was brewing between his three-year-old heir, Dona Isabella, represented by her liberal-minded mother, and his absolutist brother Don Carlos, who was invoking the Salic law to challenge her succession.

These were ongoing problems. Of more immediate importance were those of the ailing Ottoman Empire, where the sultan, Mahmud II, was seeking French and British help against the rebellious pasha of Egypt, Mehemet Ali, who had recently invaded Syria and was threatening to march on Constantinople. It was essential, in Talleyrand's view, that the French and British offer their support; otherwise the sultan would turn to Russia, opening the way to a dangerous increase in Russian influence in Turkey. Both Broglie and Palmerston saw the sense of this, but Palmerston was unable to persuade the Cabinet to agree: the British navy was still enforcing the embargo on Dutch shipping, and the Cabinet had no wish to take on further foreign commitments. The French were not prepared to act in isolation and in the end it was the tsar who came to Turkey's rescue by sending troops to the Dardanelles, thus checking Mehemet Ali's advance and forcing him to withdraw from Anatolia. A face-saving peace between the sultan and Mehemet Ali in early May brought the situation to an ostensibly happy ending, but the subsequent signing of a treaty between Russia and Turkey at Unkiar Skelessi in July decisively tilted the balance of power in the area in Russia's favour. Palmerston would later refer to his failure to support the sultan when he first asked for help as one of the biggest errors of his career.

Talleyrand never wasted time on regrets. Although he had been forthright in warning of Russia's ambitions in his private despatches, neither he nor Broglie wished to confront her openly. None of the major powers wanted conflict if they could help it. Russia was just recovering from the massive effort of her brutal repression of the Poles; Austria and Prussia were too keen to prevent the spread of revolutionary movements in their own territories to embark on unnecessary foreign adventures. With the major problem of Belgium all but solved, Europe seemed to be settling down to a period of relative stability.

The mood was reflected in London, where the plenipotentiaries of the various powers, thrown together closely by the Belgian conference, had all learned to know and appreciate one another. In his memoirs Talleyrand gives pen portraits of his diplomatic colleagues. Closest in spirit was Prince Paul Esterházy, Austrian ambassador in London since 1815. One of the richest men in Europe, his receptions rivalled Talleyrand's in magnificence, and his gaiety and ease of manner concealed a sharp intelligence and surprisingly liberal views. He delighted in Talleyrand's company, comparing his position as ambassador in London to that of the Sun King, Louis XIV: 'La France, c'est moi.' His deputy, Baron de Wessenberg, supposedly sent by Metternich to restrain the ambassador's liberal tendencies, was distinguished above all, according to Talleyrand, by his encyclopaedic knowledge of the European gossip of the past 40 years.

The Prussian minister, Baron von Bülow, married to the daughter of the Prussian foreign minister, Humboldt, was 'a man of ability and humour, of the Prussian kind; sometimes pushing adroitness to the verge of cunning'. The Russian ambassador, Prince Lieven, was 'far more capable than is generally supposed', though greatly overshadowed by his wife. Talleyrand reserved several paragraphs for this lady, acknowledging her pre-eminent position in London society, and her ability to be on intimate terms with whoever happened to be in power: 'She had spared no arts of coquetry to win over Lord Grey when he took office,' he noted, 'and I had many an opportunity of perceiving that she had to some extent succeeded.'[12]

Although depicted as rivals, Dorothea and Princess Lieven were too clever not to enjoy one another's company, and Creevey, in a letter to his stepdaughter, Mrs Ord, describes an amusing conversation between the two:

> The great subject that was handled by our Princess Lieven and the Dino was being *bored*... The Lieven's creed is that she *would not* be bored,

and the Dino's that she *could not*. The Russian avowed that the instant a person began to bore her she got up and left them, and that nothing could or should extort any civility from her at the expense of being bored; so the Dino said, 'What do you do when you stay at Windsor with the Queen?' 'Oh,' said the other, 'elle m'amuse,' which I think was very *low*... Dino said that from her infancy she had always had civility impressed upon her as the first lesson, and that from having always practised it she did not know what boring meant. She mentioned a curious fact of old (or as she said Mons'r) Talleyrand, viz. that he hated to be left alone, that he preferred the company of the most stupid companion to such solitude, and she added that when there was more than one such person, it was understood that she was to take the most stupid to herself... As the Lieven could not be shaken in her own hostility to civility, the Dino tried for a compromise in favour of *parent* or *mari* to which the Lieven made her last reply, 'J'ai un grand respect pour mon mari mais il m'incommode.'

'So that ended it,' wrote Creevey, 'but it was really very curious, and very entertaining.'[13]

12

A New Challenge

O N 25 March 1833 Talleyrand received a letter from Madame Adélaïde, announcing the approaching visit to London of her nephew, the Duc d'Orléans. As the eldest son of Louis-Philippe and heir to the French throne he would be demonstrating the continuity of the new dynasty as well as confirming the importance of the Anglo-French alliance. It was a good moment for the visit. The success of the Antwerp expedition was still fresh in people's minds; meanwhile, the Duchesse de Berry, awaiting the birth of her baby in comfortable house imprisonment, had effectively destroyed the hopes of the Carlists, as the supporters of Charles X's grandson were known. 'She has made cuckolds of them all,' Talleyrand remarked.[1] Charles X himself had left Edinburgh for Prague that winter, his departure expedited by the number of debts he left behind. Talleyrand, it was whispered, had helped to ratchet up the pressure from his creditors.

It was important for the standing of the July Monarchy that Orléans should be suitably received. 'I'm insisting both to the king and to him,' wrote Broglie to Talleyrand, 'that he should maintain the most aristocratic attitude possible and give no excuses to those who ask nothing better than to treat him as a parvenu.'[2] There were still many supporters of the Bourbons among the British aristocracy, and it needed all Dorothea's skill and social contacts to make sure he was well received. There were a few awkward moments. Lord Sefton, for instance, was persuaded to give a grand reception in the young duke's honour, but there was a full-length portrait of Charles X in his dining room and the picture had to be tactfully removed. Then there was Flahaut, a close friend of the duke's, who expected to join the royal entourage: Talleyrand, who now entertained a 'particular aversion' to him, made sure he was excluded. 'The Dino is doing everything one could wish in her anxiety that all should be right,' noted Creevey approvingly.

> The Queen of France wrote to her begging that she would be a *Mentor* to the youthful Orléans whilst here; on which account she told the Seftons *she did not dance in his presence, thinking it unbecoming the character of a Mentor*; but at the Queen's Ball when [Queen] Adelaide was asked to dance, she replied that she could not if she was the only married woman, so the Dino was asked to stand up to the difficulty, and the Mentor for once complied.[3]

Eighteen years younger than his mentor, Orléans fell slightly in love with Dorothea: good-looking, well educated and, like all heirs apparent, not always in agreement with his father, he found her a sympathetic confidante. Both he and his parents were delighted with the success of his visit. The government and the opposition went out of their way to honour him; the king and queen were at their most gracious; Talleyrand presided urbanely over all. 'I have never seen a man so considerable and so well considered,' wrote the Comte de Saint-Priest, who accompanied the royal party. 'The July Revolution is sometimes a little bourgeois, but thanks to Monsieur de Talleyrand, it has a very grand air in London. Madame de Dino also plays her part in this ensemble extremely well.'[4]

In between the parties and entertainments of the royal visit, negotiations with the king of Holland were reaching a satisfactory conclusion. Surprisingly, it was the representatives of the northern powers – Russia, Austria and Prussia – who helped bring this about. While the negotiations between Holland, Belgium, France and Britain were taking place, they continued to have informal discussions with all the parties involved, and to report back on their findings to their foreign ministries. Finally, on a visit to Berlin, Prince Lieven's second in command, Count Matusiewicz, persuaded the three northern powers to advise the king of Holland to accept a temporary settlement. This was exactly what Talleyrand had hoped for. He had done his best to calm the impetuousness of the French politicians, 'who, under pressure from the Belgians, wanted to take strong measures against Holland at the very moment when, as I suspected, the king was going to give in.'[5] He could not resist pointing out the moral in a letter to Broglie on 27 May – six days after the settlement had been signed:

> One must, it seems to me, see in these circumstances a new proof of the disadvantages of letting oneself become too carried away by exaggerated reports. If one had listened to all the information which for the last few months has been transmitted to us from all sides, we would have had to believe that Holland's resistance was insurmountable and that she was supported by the three northern powers. We can now see that these reports were more the result of personal opinions and also perhaps of inexperience, than of a profound knowledge of affairs.[6]

It was a vindication of his style of personal diplomacy and the network of good relations he had built up with his European colleagues. It would be five years before the Dutch accepted the inevitable and made their provisional treaty permanent, but from now on they and the Belgians could get on with their lives as separate nations. For all practical purposes the question of Belgium had been solved, and the success of its constitutional monarchy was proved when in 1848 it was one of the only countries in Europe that did not suffer a revolution.

The death of Talleyrand's old friend the Duc de Dalberg that April had been a new break with Talleyrand's past. 'Poor Dalberg! How much

I loved him and how much I miss him,' he wrote sadly.[7] The world he had known was changing and he was not in sympathy with the new one. Driving with him to Holland House one evening – it was 'the highest honour' to be introduced there – Mérimée asked Talleyrand whether he thought the Revolution had had a good or bad effect on the French nation. It was not a question Talleyrand was prepared to answer in a wider sense, but he deplored the loss of the style and graces of his youth: 'Before the Revolution there was wickedness but there was also elegance; there was malice, but there was also wit. Today there is only tasteless wickedness and the malice of stupidity.'[8]

There was still Montrond to remind him of the old days. Witty and wicked as ever, he continued to haunt the French embassy. Dorothea, who loathed him, would have disliked him still more if she had known he was the instigator of a spiteful trick involving her. The story was recounted by Mérimée in a letter to his old friend Henri Beyle (Stendhal), currently consul in Civitavecchia, using a simple code: Dorothea was the 'Duchesse de 10.no', or *Dix.no*; Montrond, M. de *Colline Ronde* (*colline* meaning 'hill'), or Mont Rond:

M. de Colline Ronde, on a recent visit to England, amused himself by persuading Lord Palmerston's son [in fact the son of Palmerston's mistress, Lady Cowper] that he owed it to himself to take a mistress like the d'esse de 10.no, and that he should go right ahead. At the same time he told the duchesse that for the honour of France, which she represented, she should not allow the dandy to attack her and that she should defend herself against his temerity, using the weapons nature gave her. The said dandy threw himself upon the duchesse... and was seen off with a scratched nose and the loss of half his hair. And Mephistopheles Colline Ronde laughed.[9]

The upshot, wrote Mérimée, was that the journalist, Henri de Latouche, printed the story in *Figaro*, with the characters thinly disguised, and that one of Dorothea's former lovers, Émile Piscatory, challenged Latouche to a duel. The duel ended with Latouche firing in the air, but the publicity involved did nothing to help Dorothea's reputation in the salons of the Faubourg Saint-Germain.

She had never got used to her treatment by the French press. 'For many years now,' she once wrote, 'I've agonised over insults, libels, every kind of filth, calumny and horror. Living in the same house and in the confidence of M. de Talleyrand, and moreover in an exceptionally libellous and opinionated age, how could I escape?' The only way to preserve her peace of mind, she found, was not to read the papers at all. 'I don't want to know the bad things people think of me and my friends... it's better to avoid such painful knowledge altogether.'[10]

Talleyrand was more resilient. But even he must have found it bitter that the peaceful solution of the Belgian question, achieved after so much effort, did nothing to stem the stream of abuse against him in the opposition papers. The contrast with his immense popularity in Britain was striking. 'The kind of interest and curiosity that he excites,' wrote Dorothea,

is unabated. In descending from his carriage in Kensington the other day, we saw women lifted up in the arms of their husbands so that they could see M. de Talleyrand better. His portrait, by Scheffer, is now with the print merchant, Colnaghi, to be engraved; it attracts a great deal of attention... Apropos of this portrait, it is placed at Colnaghi's next to that of M. Pitt. One of the curious who was examining the two the other day said, in showing that of Pitt: 'Here is someone who created great events; this one (indicating M. de Talleyrand) knew how to observe and profit from them.'[11]

The original of the painting had been bought at the Paris Salon by Lord Holland; it would hang with the portraits of his friends and family in the long panelled library at Holland House.

Talleyrand stayed on in London for four months after peace with Holland had been signed. His main task had been completed, and though there were other themes to follow – relations with Turkey and civil wars in Spain and Portugal – there was no immediate action to be taken. On 9 September he wrote to Broglie to ask permission for an extended leave of absence, its duration to be decided by the importance, or otherwise, of future happenings. Broglie readily agreed; Bacourt was put in charge of the embassy, and, on 24 September 1833, having delayed his departure in order to accept an invitation to stay with the king and queen at Windsor, Talleyrand set sail for France. 'On leaving London in September,' he wrote in his memoirs,

> I had more or less decided not to return. I believed I had left things in such a way that my presence was no longer necessary, and in addition, my great age, my infirmity and the state of my personal affairs, greatly disordered by my long absences, made me think that it was time to retire.[12]

He was still considering his decision when, at the beginning of November, he was urgently recalled to Paris from Valençay by Broglie and the king. Did they wish him to return to London? Even Dorothea, who knew him best, found it impossible to advise him what course to pursue. On the one hand, she knew that he dreaded the isolation, boredom and inactivity of provincial existence; on the other she knew that life in Paris, where he would be held responsible by the public for decisions in which he had no interest or say, would be impossible. Nor could he hide from himself the serious complications he would find in London, augmented by the individuals – Palmerston and Broglie – with whom he would have to deal. In fact, thought Dorothea, he understood perfectly well that he might lose everything he had achieved so miraculously in the last three years in a single throw.

Talleyrand played for time. His reply to Broglie, wrote Dorothea in her journal, was something along the following lines:

Valençay, 11 November 1833. – My dear duke, you have too good an opinion of my health, but you will always be right in having an excellent one of my friendship for you and of my devotion to the king. I cannot give you a better proof of this than by dragging my 82 years [in fact he was 80] in the middle of winter from my present repose and idleness to Paris on 4 December, which I promise to do. As for going to London, I don't see any great necessity; I am very old, someone else will do things there just as well, if not better.

They would talk in Paris, he continued, and since Broglie did him the honour of consulting him, he would tell him frankly what he thought when he learned what was happening in foreign affairs; it was all he was good for now.

But if, by some impossibility, you succeed in deluding my self-esteem enough to persuade me that I am, for a short time, indispensable, or nearly so, to your concerns, then naturally I will see it as it my duty to deal with them until they have been resolved, but after that, I shall immediately return to my den [a fine word for the splendours of Valençay] and the leisured life which is the only thing that suits me nowadays.[13]

Since Talleyrand had left London a major shift had taken place in the position of the northern powers. In October 1833 the sovereigns of Russia, Austria and Prussia signed the Convention of Münchengrätz, a treaty agreeing that any ruler threatened with revolution in his territories might call on them for armed assistance. It was no more than a return to the absolutist notions of the Holy Alliance, but in practical terms it provided an excuse for Austria to crack down on insurrections in Italy, for Russia to strengthen its hold on Turkey, and for Prussia to block the movement for democracy in its neighbouring German states. All three sovereigns declared their determination to prevent the spread of liberalism – or as they saw it, revolution – and pledged themselves to come to one another's aid should it arise in their own countries.

Although they had done nothing to prevent it, the northern powers had been piqued by France and Britain's unilateral action over Antwerp, and the Münchengrätz Convention, in Talleyrand's opinion, was their way of reasserting themselves. There was nothing overtly hostile to either country in the treaty, but it drew a line between autocratic and constitutional governments that had been blurred during the Belgian negotiations. France and Britain could do little to prevent Russia's encroachments in Turkey, and Austria's in Italy, but they had their own spheres of influence to defend: in Switzerland, where Austria was trying to prevent changes in the constitution, in newly created Belgium, and above all in the Iberian peninsula, where civil wars threatened Britain's trading interests with Portugal and the security of France's frontier with Spain. It was important to find a counterbalance to the alliance of the northern powers. The best way to do so, it seemed to Broglie and the king, was to strengthen the relationship between France and Britain by a defensive treaty against 'unprovoked aggression' by other powers. It was this they now looked to Talleyrand to negotiate.

How could Talleyrand resist the challenge? From the beginning to the end of his political career, he wrote (conveniently glossing over the Napoleonic Wars), an alliance between France and Britain had been his dearest wish, convinced as he was that 'the peace of the world, the consolidation of liberal values and the progress of civilisation could only rest on such a base'.[14] He promised to give the matter serious thought but his decision had already been made. Shortly before Christmas, preceded two days earlier by a still uncertain Dorothea, he set out for London once again.

13

The Quadruple Alliance

ONE person who did not look forward to Talleyrand's return to London was Bacourt, left in charge during his absence. Writing to Dorothea in November, he did not conceal his dismay at the prospect of 'coming under the yoke of M. de Talleyrand's bad temper once again'. 'It's no use you telling me he's grown gentle as a lamb,' he wrote;

> there is a gulf between us that can never be bridged. I can forgive his wrongs towards me, putting them down to his age, his health, the pressure of affairs; but I've determined to live with him on the basis of master and official, and never become to him what I have been before.[1]

It is uncertain what affronts Bacourt had suffered. Perhaps Talleyrand had been difficult and querulous at times; perhaps he had been unexpectedly jealous of the younger man. The same letter to Dorothea – one of the few that has survived – leaves it in no doubt that Bacourt was now her lover: he writes of the need for discretion; he calls her his angel, his beautiful lady, 'his pretty magpie', in reference to her chattering tongue. But Dorothea was a master of having her cake and eating it. She loved Bacourt, and he knew it, while accepting that Talleyrand would always be the centre of her life. Talleyrand in his turn was fond of Bacourt, and in later years took endless trouble in furthering his career. Somehow

Dorothea succeeded in smoothing over the difficulties between the two men and before long they were working together as closely as before.

During his journey to London Talleyrand had given careful thought to the best way to present the idea of a defensive treaty. The concept of 'legitimacy' had helped to re-establish the Bourbon monarchy in 1815; that of 'non-intervention' had smoothed the negotiations over Belgium. It was time, he wrote to Broglie, to find a new phrase to reassure the other powers; he suggested it should be the maintenance of 'the status quo'. Under this heading a treaty between France and Britain would balance the alliance of northern powers in a way they could not quarrel with, since they themselves were devoted to the principle of resisting change.

It was an attractive and plausible proposition, but Broglie, who was closer to public opinion in France, knew that it would never be accepted. To insist on maintaining the status quo would stir up those sections of the public – republicans and Bonapartists alike – who were still smarting from the loss of French territories after 1815 and hoping to reclaim them in the not-too-distant future. It would be better, he wrote, to leave matters vague and to find some neutral slogan which offended neither French opinion nor the northern powers.

In the event the discussion over words did not arise. Parliament was in recess over Christmas and Palmerston, who came up from the country specially to see Talleyrand, showed little enthusiasm for the plan. 'We have no objection to treaties for specific and indefinite and immediate objects,' he told him bluntly, 'but we do not much fancy treaties which are formed in contemplation of indefinite and undefined objects. We like to be free to judge of each occasion as it arises.'[2] Grey and Holland echoed the same view. But they made much of Britain's close links with France – Palmerston in even stronger terms than usual – and the king's speech in February made a special point of the relationship. 'The constant aim of my policy,' declared William IV, 'is to ensure for my people the uninterrupted enjoyment of the benefits of peace. In this I have been perfectly seconded by the good understanding so happily established between my government and that of France.'[3]

It was hard to be more positive, but the speech stopped short of mentioning a definite alliance. Neither Grey nor Palmerston wished to tie his hands unnecessarily and they had their own aims to pursue in Portugal and Spain. It looked as though the treaty which Talleyrand had hoped would be the crowning triumph of his career was not going to materialise. It was also clear that Broglie, despite having pleaded with Talleyrand to return, was continuing to deal direct with Palmerston through Granville and that Palmerston encouraged this state of affairs. Princess Lieven, a shrewd and not unsympathetic observer, summed up the situation:

He [Talleyrand] immediately discovered that the ministers would not deal with him and that all affairs were being handled between M. de Broglie and the British ambassador in Paris; that Lord Palmerston might be courteous, but told him absolutely nothing. Although he continued to receive flattering letters from the Tuileries [that is, from Madame Adélaïde], his own Cabinet left him in total ignorance of their intentions. For a man of such ability and talent, such a situation is unbearable. Madame de Dino weeps – and he no longer laughs.[4]

Dorothea might weep, but Talleyrand did not give up so easily. The Whig government was in a precarious state. The influx of radicals and Irish nationalists since the Reform Bill had diluted its authority, and the Tories were once more gathering their forces. If the government fell, Palmerston would fall with it, and under the Duke of Wellington things might take a very different turn. Nor was the ministry in France, where violent upheavals in Lyons and Marseilles had shaken public confidence, altogether secure. One of the objections put forward by Palmerston to the idea of signing a treaty with France was that the government might not last; the same point could be made by Talleyrand.

For the time being he put a brave face on his setbacks. Still lionised by society, he continued to play cards at the Travellers Club, to add rare books to his library (and present one to the British Museum) and to entertain as lavishly as ever – all this, despite the fact, recorded by Princess Lieven, that he had recently lost 100,000 francs in the funds: 'He gambles in money just as he does in politics, or rather he deals with the one just as he does the other, and for the moment neither is going well.'[5]

Things were not going well for Princess Lieven either. A political storm had blown up which for all her vaunted influence she was unable to dispel. It was an example, wrote Talleyrand in his memoirs, of Palmerston's tendency to bring his personal hatreds into public affairs. In this case he had been angered by the tsar's refusal to accept the appointment of a distinguished diplomat, Sir Stratford Canning, as British ambassador to Russia – Sir Stratford, while ambassador at Constantinople, had been highly critical of Russia's Turkish policy. 'Lord Palmerston,' wrote Talleyrand,

> replied with his usual stiffness that it was possible that a British ambassador might have displeased the tsar by conscientiously carrying out his duties and his government's instructions, but that this did not appear a sufficient motive not to appoint him to a mission to which his services entitled him and if the choice was not agreed to the British government would leave the post of ambassador to St Petersburg vacant.[6]

Confrontation had been delayed for a year while Grey's son-in-law, Lord Durham, was sent to Russia on a special mission. But Durham returned in March and neither Palmerston nor the tsar was prepared to climb down. Palmerston refused to take back Canning's nomination; the tsar refused to accept it and the embassy in St Petersburg was accordingly left in the hands of the chargé d'affaires. In Talleyrand's view, it was a mistake to insist; Britain had no intention of going to war over Turkey and there was no point in picking an unnecessary quarrel. Palmerston might argue that Canning, with his wide experience of Ottoman affairs, was the person best suited to deal with Russia over the Eastern question, but it was hard to believe that there was not an element of obstinacy involved as well.

To the very last Princess Lieven had been convinced that her influence with Grey and other members of the Cabinet would avert the nomination. Suddenly she was faced with the prospect of leaving London; sooner or later the tsar was bound to withdraw his ambassador in retaliation. After 22 years as the queen of London society, she would be forced to return to the boredom, snows and rigid court etiquette of Russian life. The truth was, as Talleyrand told her bluntly, 'It's always in the power of a minister of foreign affairs, however mediocre he may be, to get rid of an ambassador.'[7]

Talleyrand's own frustrations in dealing with Palmerston had been somewhat diminished when, on 28 March, Broglie unexpectedly resigned as foreign minister. He had done so on a point of principle; a treaty with the United States signed by his predecessor was repudiated in the Chamber of Deputies, and though not personally responsible, he felt himself honour-bound to stand down. Talleyrand respected his decision, which was typical of his strict and upright character, but was secretly relieved at his departure. The new foreign minister, Comte de Rigny had none of Broglie's authority and experience and was far more inclined to defer to his ambassador's judgement. Whether he liked it or not, Palmerston was obliged to reckon with Talleyrand once more.

The change in emphasis was quickly revealed when on 9 April Palmerston invited Talleyrand to spend the morning with him at the Foreign Office to discuss an affair which, he suggested, might be of interest to him. It concerned the problems of the Iberian peninsula, where the civil wars in Spain and Portugal had recently ended in an uneasy peace. In Spain, following the death of Ferdinand VII, his infant daughter Isabella II had come to the throne, with her mother acting as regent. In Portugal, Dom Pedro's forces had taken Lisbon on behalf of his 15-year-old daughter, Maria II, defeating his reactionary brother Dom Miguel. The new governments, constitutional in character, continued to be under threat from the reactionary claimants, Don Carlos in Spain and Dom Miguel in Portugal, and Don Carlos had now joined forces with Dom Miguel, who still controlled large areas of the countryside, to overthrow Maria II. So far Britain had taken no action, but Palmerston had recently been approached by the Portuguese and Spanish envoys in London to ask for his help in defeating the two claimants. It was important to move fast, since Carlos's troops had already entered Portugal, and the northern powers – who naturally supported the absolutist side – were waiting to intervene. 'In the presence of this simultaneous demand,' Palmerston told Talleyrand,

> the government of His Britannic Majesty believes it can no longer delay taking the action demanded by the circumstances; and I have been charged to respond to the overtures of M. de Florida Banca and M. de Sarmento [the Spanish and Portuguese envoys] by proposing a treaty between England, Spain and Portugal.[8]

This treaty, he continued, would require Spain to use all possible means to expel Carlos and Miguel from Portugal, and afterwards to withdraw her own forces. Maria's government, for its part, would support Spain in the enterprise, and undertake to grant a general amnesty in Portugal and a pension for her uncle, Miguel, when the civil war was over. Britain, meanwhile, would send ships to support the Spanish and Portuguese governments by blockading ports and cutting off rebel supplies, but would land no troops on any part of the peninsula. The treaty, which had already been drawn up, included a clause inviting France to accede to its terms, and it was this that he had invited Talleyrand to discuss.

Here was a pistol to Talleyrand's head. He had known nothing of the treaty and certainly was not prepared to sign an agreement in which France – by 'acceding' rather than 'contracting' – was to play a subsidiary role. But it was a chance to reopen his favourite project of a defensive alliance with Britain. A joint treaty such as he envisaged, he argued, would cover any actions needed to calm the troubles in the peninsula. However, rather than reject Palmerston's proposal outright, he suggested a compromise solution, whereby, if Britain still refused the idea of a joint treaty, France should become an equal partner with the other three powers in the proposed alliance.

Palmerston promised to report their conversation to the Cabinet, adding that he personally had many objections to the idea of a joint alliance. Talleyrand replied that he regretted this all the more acutely since every day, he feared, would show more clearly how necessary it was to European peace. Privately, however, he was satisfied with what he had achieved. Even if the idea of a joint treaty was rejected it could be used as leverage to force France's entry into the wider alliance suggested by Palmerston. Since this possibility had not even been discussed when the meeting began he felt that his morning had been well spent.

The Cabinet was eager to get the treaty agreed as soon as possible, and rather than be dragged into protracted discussions reluctantly accepted France's demand to join what came to be known as the Quadruple Alliance on an equal basis. Palmerston now hoped that the treaty could be agreed at once by telegraph, so that it could be signed as soon as possible in London. To his annoyance, however, the French government replied by courier, demanding a number of alterations (designed to satisfy French public opinion), which were left to Talleyrand to negotiate on the spot.

Some of the alterations Palmerston accepted without trouble, others he flatly turned down. A series of notes between him and Talleyrand during 19 and 20 April reveal his mounting impatience. 'Ma foi,' he exclaimed at one point, 'but you are difficult to deal with.' When Talleyrand, having pushed things as far as he could, at last agreed the final wording, he could not resist suggesting that a redundant clause should be erased on grounds of style. 'M de Voltaire,' he wrote, 'once said that of all the changes his friends suggested he make to his works, he never regretted what he cut.'

This was too much for Palmerston:

> What Voltaire says is true for books, but as far as treaties are concerned the contrary is the case; one could well say that many disputes between states would never have taken place if their treaties had been explained more fully. May I now send the treaty, as it is, for the approval of the king? Send me a 'yes' and quickly, for time is really short.[9]

Talleyrand laid down his arms: 'Dear Lord Palmerston – Eh bien! *Oui*.'[10]

Two days later, having been translated into their respective languages – a considerable feat in itself – the Quadruple Alliance was signed by the representatives of all four powers. It was a major achievement, completed at lightning speed and in many ways preferable to Talleyrand's plan of a joint alliance. Above all, it was an answer to the Treaty of Münchengrätz. 'I cannot believe,' wrote Talleyrand to Rigny,

> that the alliance we have just concluded, which not only strengthens our links with England but also makes Spain and Portugal, so to speak, our dependants, is not destined to command a certain respect in the cabinets of the north. They could add, if they wished to, Belgium and perhaps Switzerland to the circle of our allies – and even if they regard it as a union of countries agitated by the spirit of revolution, they will undoubtedly be more cautious about provoking attacks from a mass not only formidable in itself but in the sympathies it inspires in others.[11]

The Quadruple Alliance could thus be presented as a liberal manifesto. It was not altogether successful in its immediate aims – rebellion was crushed in Portugal, but continued for five more years in Spain. Its real importance was symbolic: by linking the four constitutional states of the West in an alliance it encouraged struggling liberal movements everywhere. Meanwhile, as Talleyrand pointed out prosaically to Rigny, it cost France nothing in terms of men or money, for the treaty did not commit her to intervene unless she wished. Palmerston might be eager to take action. With memories of Napoleon's disastrous Peninsular campaign behind them, the French were less inclined to do so.

14

A Changing Scene

⁓

THE Quadruple Alliance was the last great triumph of Talleyrand's diplomatic career. The concept had been Palmerston's; Talleyrand's achievement had been to insist on France being included and in doing so to confirm her status as a major European player. Louis-Philippe's throne, somewhat wobbly to begin with, was now solidly established. Talleyrand's aim, since the revolution of 1830, had been to win him what he called 'le droit de la cité', the right to citizenship in Europe, and this right was no longer in doubt. Despite their earlier differences, he and Palmerston had got on well during the negotiations: one historian described their exchanges as 'a delightful exhibition of diplomatic technique between two masters.'[1] Only a few weeks before, Palmerston had written to Granville to 'contradict the absurd rumours that there was any ill feeling between himself and Talleyrand.'[2]

The situation was about to deteriorate, thanks largely to Talleyrand's own behaviour. The treaty had been intended to be kept secret until it had been ratified in Paris, Lisbon and Madrid, but Talleyrand, with studied indiscretion, disclosed it to Lieven and Esterházy only three days later. Despite the Quadruple Alliance he was anxious to stay on good terms with the northern powers, and moreover had no wish to be associated with Palmerston's quarrel with the tsar. It was perhaps not surprising that Palmerston was annoyed by what he saw as Talleyrand's deviousness and that he showed it in his increasingly offhand manner. On one occasion, Grey was so embarrassed by his discourtesy towards the ambassador that he ran down the staircase after Dorothea, who happened to be visiting him next day, to assure her that Palmerston meant no ill will to Talleyrand and to ask her to make his excuses for him. 'I promise you to tell Monsieur de Talleyrand that Lord Palmerston is as innocent as an unborn child,' replied Dorothea in her charming, slightly accented English, 'but I don't believe a word of it.'[3]

'It's all very well,' she wrote crossly in her journal, 'for M. de Talleyrand to say that he gets through work easily, that he speaks and writes good French, but he's limited, presumptuous; his nature is arrogant, and his character dishonest.'[4]

Talleyrand had dealt with monsters in his time: the horrors of the Revolution, the corruption of the Directory, the destructive wars of Napoleon had left him with few expectations about human nature. Palmerston might be brusque and abrasive, but he belonged to the civilised world. Whatever their personal differences, their aims were more or less similar, and the solid achievements of Belgian independence and the Quadruple Alliance were their joint work. He was not going to spoil his last few months in London by falling out with him.

Talleyrand's memoirs, which cover the four years of his embassy in London, come to an end with the signing of the Quadruple Alliance. His remaining time there is recorded in his despatches and letters, put together by Bacourt when he came to edit the memoirs many years later. Dorothea's journal, on the other hand, describes this period more fully than any other during her stay. It seemed as though she had just got into her stride. 'When I first came here, four years ago,' she wrote, 'I had no happy memories of the past, no interest in the present, no thoughts for the future; I asked no more of each succeeding day than a little distraction.'[5] Like Talleyrand, she was good at hiding her feelings, and few people would have suspected the underlying melancholy – what Talleyrand called the '*allemanderie*' (Germanness) – behind her delightful and lively exterior. But her four beautiful years in London, she wrote, had passed with a rapidity which could only be explained by the interest of events and the particular reasons for happiness – perhaps she was thinking of Bacourt – which she found there. She should have written of them earlier; it was only during her last few months that she took to recording them almost daily.

She writes of seeing the young Princess Victoria, nearly 15 and small for her age, but already possessing the royal capacity to stand still for long periods; of the queen's forthcoming journey to Germany to see her family and the loudly expressed delight of William IV at the prospect of returning to his 'bachelor' amusements during her absence; of the beauty of London in May:

> The multitude of squares, so green, so flowering, those parks so rich in vegetation, verandas suspended from the houses and covered with flowers, climbing plants which carpet the walls of the houses up to the second floor, all this is so delicious to the eye that one regrets the sun a little less, since it would take away something of its freshness.[6]

She takes pleasure in English eccentricity. Here she is, for instance, on the old Marchioness of Salisbury:

> She went, last Sunday, to church, something which happens very rarely; the preacher, speaking of original sin, said that Adam excused himself by crying, 'Lord, the woman tempted me!' At this quotation, which she appeared to have heard for the first time, Lady Salisbury jumped up from her seat, saying 'Shabby fellow indeed.'[7]

She complains of embarrassing visitors. Montrond turns up from Paris:

> His quick and incisive wit is still the same; and though no one could be less boring, I find myself overcome by the same kind of uneasiness one

feels in the presence of a venomous being... The charm which fascinated M. de Talleyrand for so long has worn off, leaving a feeling of oppression and fatigue.[8]

Napoleon's brother, Jérôme, former king of Westphalia, arrives in London and seeks an audience with William IV – to whom all Bonapartes are anathema. The king's response is characteristically direct: 'Let him go to the devil.' This does not prevent Jérôme from appearing in a box at the opera, sitting in the front seat, with two courtiers standing at attention behind him as though he were still a reigning monarch.

Above all, she watches the politics of the day. Both Grey and Wellington are her confidants. Two years after the triumph of the Reform Bill, Grey was exhausted and discouraged. Disputes over Ireland and the question of tithes – imposed on the Catholic peasantry for the benefit of the Anglican Church – had split Parliament. It was only with difficulty that he had been restrained from resigning earlier in the year: 'The conservatives as well as the radicals are already disputing his succession; it is impossible not to see that the moment is critical for everyone.'[9]

Dorothea, conservative at heart, had never approved of the Reform Bill. She felt that only Grey, among the Whigs, stood between the country and outright revolution. Her sympathies were far more with Wellington, and she made no secret of her admiration in her journal:

> There is an admirable good sense and directness in his judgement...
> he forgets nothing, exaggerates nothing; and if there is something a bit
> clipped, dry and military in his conversation, it is nonetheless attractive
> in its naturalness, accuracy and good taste.[10]

Returning from Ampthill, the Hollands' country house in Bedfordshire, on 22 May, she and Talleyrand heard the news that the tsar was withdrawing his ambassador from London. The tsar had sweetened the pill by appointing Lieven as tutor to his eldest son and his wife as a lady-in-waiting to the empress, but this was small consolation to Princess Lieven, who was distraught at the thought of leaving all her friends. Grey, who called on Dorothea two days later, was obviously upset by what had happened; he was still on vaguely amorous terms with Princess Lieven, and found it hard to deal with her reproaches. He insisted, however, that the breach was not caused by any bad feeling on Palmerston's side. 'I could see,' wrote Dorothea, 'that he was anxious that the seeds of bitterness between M. de Talleyrand and Lord Palmerston should not germinate.'[11]

The diplomatic scene was changing. The Esterházys left for Vienna that same month, taking much of its grandeur and gaiety with them. 'Prince Esterházy came to make his goodbyes yesterday,' wrote Dorothea. 'He was visibly moved at leaving M. de Talleyrand, who was equally affected; one does not separate from someone of his age without a feeling of concern.'[12] Meanwhile, one of Dorothea's cousins, Count Medem, was being sent from Paris to take over as Russian chargé d'affaires. Writing from Paris to her friend Lady Cowper (Palmerston's mistress and later his wife), Madame de Flahaut expressed her disapproval of the choice. Medem, she declared, was 'a poisonous little wasp, a fanatical Russian, an enemy to Poland, and to sum up everything in a single phrase a first cousin of Madame de Dino.'[13] This could only be to Britain's disadvantage, she added, since it was not in her interests that Russia and France should be friends.

The Lievens left London two months later after a round of farewell dinners, from most of which Palmerston was pointedly excluded. Since he frequently worked till midnight at the Foreign Office, he was probably happy to escape. As foreign secretary, however, he was obliged to invite the Lievens to a diplomatic dinner for the king's birthday, at which the departing ambassadress was seated on his right. Dorothea was on the other side. 'He was chilly on the right and breezy on the left,' she recorded, and obviously ill at ease, though his embarrassment was not all increased by the fact that he was not in his drawing room ready to receive the ladies as they arrived, but came in afterwards without making the slightest excuse.[14]

Dorothea had grown close to Princess Lieven over the past few months, the two women united in their loathing of Palmerston, 'that mule', as the princess described him. A group of London's leading hostesses, headed by the Duchess of Sutherland, formed a committee to offer a farewell present to Princess Lieven. Dorothea, as a foreigner, could not subscribe, but, flatteringly, they asked her to compose a suitable inscription for their gift – a bracelet set with a large pearl – and her words, translated into English, were duly engraved inside it: 'Testimony of regard, regret and affection presented to the Princess Lieven on her departure by some English ladies of her particular acquaintance.'[15]

Socially, the Lievens' departure was a great loss to London's diplomatic life; politically it made no real difference. Medem proved perfectly capable of replacing Lieven in London and Bligh, the British chargé d'affaires in St Petersburg, was well able to represent his country's interests there. The underlying problem, of how to deal with Russia's ambitions in the Dardanelles, remained unsolved, the outlines perhaps a little starker than before. Nineteen years later the conflict of interests over Turkey between Russia on the one side and France and Britain on the other would come to a head with the Crimean War.

On 9 July, Grey resigned as prime minister. The excuse was a disagreement over Ireland but he had long been seeking a way out. He was 70 years old, and having carried his party through the storms of the Reform Bill and its aftermath was eager to escape to his beloved estates in Northumberland. The news brought a moment of hope to Dorothea: if Grey was resigning, surely Palmerston would be too. Unfortunately, this did not follow and the new prime minister, Lord

Melbourne (incidentally Lady Cowper's brother), showed no sign of replacing him. But she took comfort from the fact that the king, who respected Grey, disliked Melbourne intensely and that the new ministry was unlikely to last long.

Talleyrand, who had sent the news to Rigny by telegraph, followed it up with a longer despatch on 15 July. Melbourne was planning the minimum of changes in his Cabinet and he had received assurances from Lord Duncannon, Melbourne's successor as home secretary, that the good relations between Britain and France would remain unaltered. 'This,' he wrote, 'is the essential point for us and should guide our policy, at least until other circumstances, which it would be imprudent to prejudge, make it necessary to modify it.'[16]

Rigny's answer, dated 17 July, had equally dramatic news to impart. Soult, the French prime minister, had resigned that morning, and the king was considering a Napoleonic marshal, Comte Gérard, as his successor, though nothing had yet been decided. His letter was written in a trembling hand: 'Madame de Dino will be cleverer than Champollion [the scholar of Egyptian hieroglyphics] if she manages to decipher this, as I have a fever at the moment.'[17] Even the French foreign minister, it seemed, recognised Dorothea's role as Talleyrand's chief adviser.

Talleyrand was now planning to take a leave of absence at the end of August. Would he return? There had been nothing of vital importance to discuss since the signing of the Quadruple Alliance – though the violent behaviour of the liberals in Spain, where priests had been massacred and churches pillaged, cast doubt on the virtues of their progressive government. Dorothea describes Talleyrand as torn between ambition and a sense of failing powers. Her personal opinion was that he should retire while he was still on top of things. She foresaw nothing but trouble in the changes of regime in France and Britain and had been struck by Grey's words in his speech of resignation:

When one has kept one's health and one's faculties one may still at an
advanced age usefully occupy oneself with public affairs. But, in critical
times like the present, a degree of attention, activity is required which
belongs only to the prime of life and not to its decline.[18]

She quoted these words in a letter she wrote to Talleyrand; well schooled
in drafting his despatches, she found it easier to express herself in
writing:

I have a serious duty towards you which I never feel more acutely than
when your glory is at stake. I irritate you a little sometimes by talking,
and then I stop before I have said all I think. So let me write to you and
please forgive anything I say which annoys you because it is my love for
you which drives me to say it.

I do not claim to be very clever but I feel I cannot be wrong when I
am thinking of you whom I know so well and whose troubles and difficulties I am so well placed to understand. It is only after much reflection
that I urge you now to leave public life and to retire from a scene on
which society in disarray is playing such a dismal part. Do not remain
any longer in a post in which you are bound to find yourself asked to
destroy all that you have worked so hard to achieve.

She pointed out the woes of Britain: a government agitated by party
spirit; a weak king; a presumptuous and arrogant foreign minister; a
new diplomatic corps 'as impudent as it is vulgar'. As for the government
he represented: 'pettiness, indiscretion, vanity and intrigue dominate
everything in Paris.' Grey had chosen the right moment to leave; it was
time for Talleyrand to follow his example:

You did not come here four years ago to make your fortune, your career,
your reputation; all these were secure long ago. You did not come out
of love for those who are ruling your country; you like them as little as

you respect them. You came with no other object than to render a great service to your country at a moment when its very foundations were shaken. At your age it was a perilous adventure! To reappear after fifteen years of retirement when the tempest was at its height and to calm it was a great undertaking. You have accomplished it; let that be enough... Declare you are old before people find you aged; say simply, nobly to the world, 'The hour has struck.'[19]

Talleyrand must have weighed her words – he kept a copy of Grey's speech in his pocket book – but he gave no outward sign of his intentions. Perhaps he had not yet decided himself. But it was plain that both the king and Palmerston were expecting him to leave for good. 'Last year,' wrote Dorothea,

the king of England said to M. de Talleyrand on his departure to the Continent, 'When are you coming back?' The year before, he said to him, 'I have commanded my ambassador in Paris to tell your government that I count on keeping you here.' This year he says, 'When are you going?' It seems to me that one can see, in such different responses, a trace of *Palmerstonian* influence.[20]

Palmerston, as foreign secretary, gave a farewell dinner before Talleyrand left for what was still termed a leave of absence. 'He didn't give himself much trouble over the party,' noted Dorothea; 'there were only, beside Mrs Petre, a few inferior diplomats; nobody English of any distinction; none of our particular friends. It was no more than a sop to his conscience, and a guilty conscience at that.'

She amused herself by teasing him at dinner:

He thought that he ought to show himself extremely desirous of our prompt return. I took him at his word, saying I could go even further than that, and that I thought M. de Talleyrand might not leave at all. He looked quite stupefied at first, then pulling back from the brink, began repeating that a change of air was necessary, indispensable, that he needed to renew himself physically and morally; in fact he wanted nothing more than to see the last of us as soon as possible.[21]

15

Time to Go

E VEN though Talleyrand had not decided whether he would return to London in the autumn there was a feeling of finality about his leave-taking. He was particularly sad to say goodbye to Lord Holland. 'The truth is,' he had told him after leaving for France the previous year,

> that I miss England greatly. People show me continual marks of kindness. The life I live here suits me. Even the climate during the winter does me no harm. There are a number of people of whom I am especially fond and you are at the top of the list.[1]

He had always been grateful to Holland for counting him as '*un des vôtres*' (one of yours) in the charmed and exclusive circle of the Whig aristocracy;[2] it was a title, he told him, bestowed on him by Fox and one which he was proud to bear. In fact, despite his affection for Holland and his friends, he was no longer much in sympathy with the Whigs. He believed in a constitutional monarchy, but the Reform Bill, he felt, had taken democracy too far. 'We all know that his partialities are with Wellington and not with us,' wrote Palmerston revealingly to Granville; 'that he considers us all as a set of dangerous Radicals who have brought our own country to the brink of Revolution.'[3]

On 20 August 1834, Talleyrand left London. It was almost exactly four years since he had arrived there, decked out with a tricolour cockade, with the aim of making the July Revolution respectable. He had succeeded in doing so triumphantly and to all intents and purposes his task was done. But it would be some time before he could finally accept it. It is not easy to sign one's own death warrant, as one of his biographers remarked, and his next few months in France would be spent in debating whether or not to resign.

Dorothea, who left a few days later, was convinced that his departure would be final:

> There is always something solemn and singularly painful in doing something for the last time, in leaving, in saying goodbye, when one is 80 years old. I feel that he also had this sentiment; I'm sure that I had it for him... I felt like saying to him as I had said to Mme de Lieven: 'I weep for my own departure in yours.'[4]

Travelling to Dover on 24 August, Dorothea was touched by her reception at the various coaching inns along the way. Everyone had been warned of her coming; people 'even of the most inferior kind' spoke warmly of her and Talleyrand, and expressed their desire to see them back in Britain. At Dover a French packet boat was waiting: the sky was blue, the sea was calm. 'Goodbye then to England,' she wrote sadly in her journal, 'but not to the memory of the four happy years I spent there... Goodbye to that hospitable country, which I leave with nothing but regret and gratitude.'[5]

For Dorothea, who had enjoyed such a brilliant success in London, it was a genuine sacrifice to return to France. Not only would she be leaving Bacourt behind, but she would be facing a largely hostile society in Paris. The majority of the aristocracy there were legitimist at heart and considered Louis-Philippe and his court rather bourgeois. They kept themselves to themselves in the salons of the Faubourg Saint-Germain, where Dorothea, because of her relationship with Talleyrand, would never be fully accepted, and where the malice of the Flahauts – who were furious at being denied the London embassy – made many social gatherings an ordeal. ('It seems,' said Talleyrand, when someone remarked on Flahaut's attitude, 'that I haven't brought him up very well.'[6]) In these circumstances she was happiest in the country, at her own chateau of Rochecotte or at Valençay, where Talleyrand, after a brief stay in Paris, had withdrawn to consider his future.

The two people most anxious that Talleyrand should return to London were Louis-Philippe and Madame Adélaïde. With the departure of the masterful Broglie, Louis-Philippe was once more largely in control of foreign affairs, and he and his sister still had total faith in Talleyrand. The fact that he was on bad terms with Palmerston was unimportant since even from the French side of the Channel it was clear that Melbourne's government was not going to last. Meanwhile, Talleyrand, wrote Dorothea, could not be *'plus à la mode'* (more in fashion) with the royal family, and the young Duc d'Orléans had promised to visit them at Valençay.

Valençay, one of the great estates of France, which had somehow survived the Revolution, had been the gift of Napoleon to Talleyrand as a place where he could entertain with a splendour suited to France's leading statesman. It had remained his, even during his years of disgrace with the emperor, a magnificent Renaissance chateau with some 40,000 acres of surrounding land. A visitor, Prosper de Barante, describes his impressions of staying there:

> Here I am in this great chateau where everything is magnificently hospitable, and dispensed with an aristocratic richness of which there is no longer any other example in France. It has a park of 300 arpents [roughly 240 acres] with troops of deer... There are huge forests, intersected as though one were in the Bois de Boulogne, by avenues where you can walk as easily as in a garden... There is a population of every kind of staff, a doctor, an almoner, a tutor, musicians, business advisers; there are rich

furnishings, marbles, paintings, engravings, a library of 10,000 books, in fact everything one hears about in the great houses of England.[7]

It was a house which demanded company and it soon filled up with visitors: writers, politicians, friends from Britain, and on 27 October, as promised, the Duc d'Orléans and his entourage. No member of the French royal family had visited the chateau since the seventeenth century, and the whole countryside was *en fête* to greet him. Entertaining royalty could be a strain for both sides, but Dorothea dispensed with formality on the first evening by taking up her needlework after dinner as she would on any family occasion, and the party broke up into little groups, some talking, some playing cards, to the great relief of the young prince. Of course, there was a round of public entertainments for him – concerts, balls, illuminations, deputations of local dignitaries – but for Dorothea the most interesting moment was a conversation she had with him at dinner on his second evening.

'Your uncle,' he said, 'tells me that he thinks we have extracted everything from England she has to give; that London is no longer the place in which to deal with great affairs; that they should be discussed in Paris, under the aegis of my father.'

'That is certainly M. de Talleyrand's opinion,' said Dorothea, 'because your father's skill and wisdom have inspired confidence in Europe, while the reverse is true of England, whose recent politics' – she was referring to the Reform Bill – 'have aroused general distrust.'

His father, continued the prince, was eager for Talleyrand to return to London, but he himself had spoken to the king before coming, saying that he thought this would be impossible. Dorothea agreed that it would be difficult.

'But, you, Madame,' asked the prince, 'what would you like?'

'Whatever is agreeable to your father, Monseigneur; if M. de Talleyrand does not go back to London, it will be because he has assured himself that, in the actual circumstances, he cannot be of use. Personally, I like

England very much; I'm attached to it by a thousand links of gratitude and admiration, above all the kindness of the queen, and the friendship of Lord Grey and the Duke of Wellington; but there are some friends one does not lose by leaving, and in years to come I hope to repay those I had in England for all their kindness to me during my four years there.'

'But if he left the embassy,' mused the prince, 'what would M. de Talleyrand do?'

'He would do whatever pleases the king,' said Dorothea; 'if His Majesty wishes to see him, he will go to Paris to pay him homage; if His Majesty allows him to repose himself he will stay in retirement, for his legs, as you see, are extremely weak and painful; in a word, Monseigneur, he will always be the devoted servant of the king.'[8]

On this loyal note the conversation ended. But it was clear that the Duc d'Orléans (who incidentally was a friend of Flahaut's) was opposed to the idea of Talleyrand's return to London. Since Dorothea secretly shared his opinion, she did nothing to contradict him.

A few weeks before the Duc d'Orléans's visit the romantic novelist George Sand, who had a house nearby, had called at Valençay with a little group of friends, including her lover, Alfred de Musset. Dorothea had returned home from riding to find them there, and had obligingly shown them round, though she found the novelist, who did most of the talking, rather tiresome. Three weeks later, an article by Sand appeared in the *Journal des débats*, which, though it did not mention them by name, was obviously a description of Valençay and its owner: 'that octogenarian fox... who for 60 years has played with crowns and peoples on the chessboard of the universe.'

Even by the standards of other opposition journalists, its portrait of Talleyrand (whom the novelist had only glimpsed through a window) was staggeringly offensive; it is worth quoting, if only to give an idea of the kind of abuse to which he was subject throughout his career – the reverse side of the admiration he enjoyed in the courts and chancelleries of Europe.

That upper lip, convex and wrinkled like that of a cat, united to a lower one, large and drooping as that of a satyr, a mixture of dissimulation and lasciviousness; those features, flabby and rounded, indications of suppleness of character; that disdainful crease in a pronounced forehead; that arrogant nose and reptile's glance: so many contrasts in one human face reveal a man born for great vices and petty actions. Never has that heart experienced a generous emotion; never has the idea of loyalty crossed that active mind; the man is an exception in nature, a monstrosity so rare that the human race, even in despising him, experiences a kind of imbecile admiration.

Dorothea did not escape. Sand describes being met by a nymph-like figure, dressed in white like a young girl:

Ah! Now I realise, it is the duchess! People say… don't repeat it, spare my imagination such hideous scenes and horrible suspicions. This old man dares to think of such a profanation; but this woman is too beautiful, it's impossible. If rampant debauchery and sordid avarice can exist in such seductive beings and can hide under such a pure exterior, let me ignore it, let me deny it.[9]

Such moral indignation was hard to reconcile with Sand's own hectic love life, and even she confessed later that she was ashamed of her '*boutade*' (outburst). This did not prevent her from reprinting it in a collection of her essays, since, according to her, one should never take back an opinion, however displeasing it might be.

Talleyrand, as usual, remained outwardly unmoved. A lifetime of being criticised had left him, if not impervious, at least resigned to press attacks. In any case he was in good company. The ridicule and personal insults endured by the king – most famously caricatured as a pear ('*le roi poire*'), his fat jowls and tapering head supposedly resembling that fruit – were on a far greater scale, and Talleyrand at least had never been the target of the assassination attempts which punctuated Louis-Philippe's reign. Talleyrand had no great respect for some of the king's ministers, but he had an enormous admiration for the king himself. He regarded him as the most enlightened statesman of his age, and as we have seen had devoted the last four years to confirming his position in Europe. In Louis-Philippe he saw the embodiment of the constitutional monarchy which he had always regarded as the best hope for France.

The trust and respect that existed between the king, Madame Adélaïde and Talleyrand were never shown more clearly than in the letters they exchanged that autumn, when Talleyrand was deciding whether or not to retire. He had been stung by Orléans's opinion that he could no longer be of any use in Britain, and had heard that the mischief-making Flahauts had been repeating the duke's remarks. At the same he had suffered a major loss with the death of one of his oldest loves and confidantes, Princess Tyszkiewicz, niece of the last king of Poland. First encountered in Warsaw, when Talleyrand accompanied Napoleon there in 1807, she had remained so devoted to him and Dorothea that she had her own apartments at Valençay and had asked to be buried there.

Talleyrand was deeply shaken by this loss; it may have been the final factor in deciding him to retire. On 13 November, yielding at last to Dorothea's entreaties, he sent an official letter of resignation to the foreign minister. Dorothea, losing no time when she heard of his decision, had composed the first draft in half an hour. The letter was addressed simply to the foreign minister, with no specific name attached. The government was undergoing one of its periodic upheavals; Rigny had resigned with the ministry and no new foreign minister had yet been found.

Writing to Madame Adélaïde the previous day, Talleyrand had warned her of his decision. 'I have to believe,' he wrote a little bitterly,

> that the king will be disposed to accept it, Monseigneur the Duc d'Orléans having told me that, in his opinion, I could no longer be of use in London. He is right, for I am old, I am infirm, I am saddened by the rapidity with

which I see my generation disappearing. Belonging to another age, I feel myself becoming a stranger to the present one.[10]

Madame Adélaïde replied by courier the next day. She was devastated at the idea of Talleyrand retiring. The king was still struggling to form a new ministry:

In this cruel position, my dear prince, you surely do not wish to add to his trouble and embarrassments by persisting in your resolution to resign. I cannot express the pain it gives him; in the name of your attachment to him and your friendship for me, I ask you to suspend your decision for the moment, to say no more about the letter to the minister of foreign affairs, to wait for new combinations and to help us with your counsels.

She suggested that if London was too far for Talleyrand, he might go to Vienna, where he could be of equal use to France. She also told him that the king had taken advantage of the absence of a foreign minister to retrieve Talleyrand's letter from the ministry before anyone had seen it. 'It is still in his hands unopened; it would give him too much pain to read it.'[11] She implored him to think again.

Talleyrand, however, had made up his mind. It would not be possible, he told her, to go to Vienna, where he had represented the Bourbons at the Congress of Vienna and where Charles X, rather than being a private citizen as in Britain, was a frequent visitor at court. London was out of the question; his health was not equal to it. 'I would be inconsolable however,' he wrote,

if I thought that my resignation would be in any way harmful to the interests of the king, but in that respect, at least, I have no fears. For two months the newspapers of every country have been preparing the public for it, and for a long time it's been said in Paris, as in London, Petersburg and Berlin, that since the retirement of Lord Grey I have been thinking seriously of my own. Everyone knows it's the personality of Lord Palmerston, the current tendencies of the British government, my great age and the weakness of my legs that have decided me. – My retirement will therefore be a surprise to no one.[12]

Still Madame Adélaïde persisted. Implicitly apologising for the Duc d'Orléans's discourtesy, she told him that he was now united with her and the king in begging him to change his mind. The news that Melbourne's government had fallen on 16 November gave her fresh hope that he would do so. The king added his own entreaties. 'My dear prince,' he wrote,

> I very much want you to come back to Paris as soon as possible, for I am anxious to talk to you about everything that has happened here [the change of ministry] and is now happening in England. I am convinced that only you can guarantee and consolidate that great work of uniting our two countries and of conserving the peace and security of Europe which you have carried out till now with such success. I hope that these powerful motives will lead you to renounce a decision which has so greatly pained me; I await your confirmation of this with the most eager impatience.[13]

Talleyrand was well pleased at the news of Melbourne's fall, which would bring Wellington and the Tories back to power. It may have been enough to make him hesitate, for it was not till five days later, in a letter whose formal language did not conceal the emotion behind it, that he confirmed his decision to the king:

> Your Majesty will pardon my delay in thanking him for his new kind-nesses, his confidence in me – I almost dare to say his friendship. I wish I could give a better answer, but I cannot ignore the serious warnings given me during the sad ceremony [the funeral of Princess Tyszkiewicz] in which I have just taken part. It has given me courage to persevere

in a resolution of which the only really painful aspect is my sorrow at displeasing the king. He will forgive me when he consents to remember the devotion with which, despite my great age, I have served him for the last four years, and will make a little allowance for me too now that the loss of my old friends, and the weight of my years, no longer allows my actions to correspond to my zeal. Thanks to you, sire, I have obtained a place for the July Revolution in the family of European nations. My work is completed and I now have the right, as well as the need, to insist upon retiring.

If he had anything to add to this simple truth, he continued, it would be that he had always honoured the Duke of Wellington, who alone could stop Britain from following its present downward path. But he could not go back to London now without appearing to be a supporter of the Tories:

I have never been a party man; I have never wanted to be one, and that has been my strength. When, four years ago, I left for England, I was in the eyes of France, that France so severe in its national susceptibilities, the man of France. Today, I would appear to be the man of Wellington. The king, in his indulgent kindness towards me, forgets my great age; he forgets that an octogenarian is not permitted to be imprudent, for what makes the faults of old age so sad is that they are irreparable.[14]

Louis-Philippe's reply sounded a note of real emotion too, though even now he did not give up hope that Talleyrand would change his mind:

I have never seen anything more perfect, nobler, more honourable or better expressed than the letter I have just received from you. I am profoundly touched by it. It costs me a great deal to accept the justice of most of your arguments against returning to London but I am too sincere, too much a friend to my friends, not to recognise that you are right. All the same, to carry frankness further, I'm afraid that the grief you are experiencing may have made you exaggerate the weight of your years and the warning signs you say you feel. Believe me when I say that the more I appreciate your great services to me and to France, the more I feel that there are those that only you can render, and you surely cannot conceal from myself how much your resolution, however well founded, adds to my troubles. It is impossible to make any plans before the new ministry in England is decided... It is for this reason, my dear prince, that I urgently wish you to come to Paris as soon as possible. I am impatient to hear you and to be heard by you; I need the benefit of your experience and above all of the advice which your enlightened friendship makes so precious. It gives me pleasure to repeat that you must always count upon mine and on all the sentiments which I have held towards you for so long.[15]

Talleyrand came up to Paris. He debated with Louis-Philippe on the implications of the situation in Britain, and the problems of his own new ministry in France, but he did not change his mind about resigning. On 7 January 1835, the former foreign minister, Sébastiani, now fully recovered from his stroke, was appointed as the new ambassador to London. Honoré Daumier, well known for his biting political cartoons, published a lithograph of him and Talleyrand in the satirical magazine *La caricature*. It showed two figures in invalid carriages crossing paths on the road between Paris and Calais, Talleyrand recognisable from his accompanying crutch. The caption below it read simply: 'Apoplexy going to replace Paralysis in London.'

Epilogue

T ALLEYRAND'S embassy in London was his swansong, to which he had brought all the talents and experience of a lifetime. His place in history had already been assured by his role in saving France at the Congress of Vienna. Dorothea had been right when she said that he had not needed to come to England in his old age. He had done so, partly perhaps from his desire to be at the centre of events once more, but also out of loyalty to Louis-Philippe and the new monarchy created by the July Revolution. Like Louis-Philippe he knew that peace in Europe was essential to the stability of the new regime. When the revolution in Belgium broke out the two of them knew that whatever the demands of French public opinion, the other powers would never let France reclaim it. The long and complex negotiations which had led to its establishment as an independent and neutral kingdom had ensured that France had, if not a subject neighbour, at least one which could not threaten her security. Without the good relations that France had built up with Britain the other powers would never have agreed to its creation. There had been several moments when Europe trembled on the brink of going to war in support of the king of Holland. Troubles elsewhere – the rebellion in Poland, insurrections in Germany and Italy – had helped to distract their attention, but the steadiness of the Anglo-French alliance and the common front it presented had been the most important factors in keeping the peace.

Louis-Philippe and Talleyrand had started from a perilous position. The first two years of Louis-Philippe's reign had been interrupted by insurrections from every side: legitimists seeking the return of the Bourbons, Bonapartists frustrated at France's failure to recapture former glories, republicans who felt that the Revolution had stopped short of its aims. Talleyrand, representing France at the conference of the European powers, needed all the weight of his reputation, all the grandeur of his social position, to counteract the bad impression made by the disturbances at home. The skilful navigation of Louis-Philippe had brought France through its domestic troubles; Talleyrand had held the pass by maintaining his country's dignity in the eyes of the other European powers.

It was only now, at the moment of his retirement, that Talleyrand began to get the appreciation he deserved. For once, the opinions of the press were favourable. 'No one contested the success of his mission,' writes his biographer, Emmanuel de Waresquiel. 'They wrote of his "courage", his "daring", his "patriotism"... So great was his popularity that people stopped in the street before his carriage to raise their hats to him.'[1] On 12 December, when he attended the inauguration of Thiers as a member of the Académie française, the whole audience stood up to greet him when he entered the hall. 'It is impossible to describe the effect he produced!' wrote Dorothea.[2]

In London Talleyrand's success had never been in doubt. Perhaps no ambassador before or since has won more golden opinions. It had been a time too when, as Talleyrand remarked, Dorothea's talents had blossomed to their fullest extent. She had won the hearts of the notoriously exclusive English aristocracy. Princess Lieven, perhaps, had been more respected; Dorothea was cleverer, more subtle, more appealing. She had also been Talleyrand's greatest support, conscious of his every mood, solicitous of his health, finely attuned to the political questions of the day – though her decidedly conservative views were said, by the Flahauts at least, to have influenced him against the Whig reforms. She had certainly been more hostile than he was to the Reform Bill. She was also more snobbish: Talleyrand respected power and talent wherever they occurred; for her they were only acceptable when accompanied by rank. Brought up in the courts of Germany, she had not been exposed to the social upheavals of the French Revolution or the concept of a 'career open to all talents' under Napoleon.

Talleyrand died at the rue Saint-Florentin in Paris in 1838, devotedly attended by Dorothea and reconciled to the Church at the very end. Louis-Philippe and Madame Adélaïde came to say goodbye to the man who had served them so well. 'It is a great honour that the king does to this house in coming here today,' said Talleyrand, and mindful of etiquette even on his deathbed, presented all those present, including the doctor and the valets, to the king.[3]

Greville, recording the event in his diary, looked back fondly on Talleyrand's four years in London:

> During the period of his embassy in England I lived a good deal with him, his house being always open to me and I dined there *en famille* whenever I pleased. Nothing could be more hospitable, more urbane and kind than he was; and it was fine to see after his stormy youth and middle age, after a lifetime spent in the very tempest and whirlwind of political agitation, how tranquilly and honourably his declining years ebbed away... The years he passed here were probably the most peaceful of his life and they served to create for him a reputation altogether new and such as to cancel out all former recollections. His age was venerable, his society was delightful, and there was an exhibition of conservative wisdom, of 'moderate and healing counsels', in all his thoughts, words and actions very becoming to his age and station, vastly influential from his sagacity and experience, and which presented him to the eyes of men as a statesman like Burleigh or Clarendon for prudence, temperance and discretion.[4]

It was a perceptive tribute from a shrewd observer of the contemporary scene. A modern writer, Roberto Calasso, in his fascinating study, *The*

Ruin of Kasch, describes Talleyrand as the master of ceremonies of his age, contriving to legitimise political change (except in the Terror, when reason ceased to reign) from the National Assembly to the Directory, from the Consulate to the Napoleonic Empire, from the restoration of the Bourbons to their overthrow in 1830. With the accession of Louis-Philippe he once more helped to usher in a new regime and ensure its acceptance by the other great powers. He was an old man at the time and his embassy in London would be his last appearance on the European stage. But he played his part with his customary skill, making the interests of France, as he claimed he had done throughout his life, his first concern.

Notes

Author's Note

1 Orieux, 762.
2 Greville, ed. Lloyd, 123.
3 Arbuthnot, ii, 393.

Prologue

1 Barère, ii, 25.
2 Talleyrand, i, 74.
3 Kelly, *Women of the French Revolution*, 3.
4 Cooper, 69.
5 Waresquiel, 222.
6 Bernard, 141.
7 Lacour-Gayet, i, 169.
8 Ibid., iii, 333.
9 Burney, ii, 49–50.
10 Talleyrand, i, 221.
11 Ibid., 118.
12 Lacour-Gayet, i, 179.
13 Talleyrand, i, 230.

Chapter 1 · The July Revolution

1 Talleyrand, iii, 332.
2 Sainte-Beuve, 63.
3 Cooper, 303.
4 Lacour-Gayet, iii, 445.
5 Kelly, *The Young Romantics*, 43.
6 Castelot, 635.
7 Waresquiel, 756.
8 Talleyrand, iii, 337.
9 Ibid., 332.

Chapter 2 · Ambassador in London

1 Waresquiel, 755.
2 Greville, ed. Reeve, ii, 44.
3 Talleyrand, iii, 451.
4 Ibid., 454.
5 Waresquiel, 756.
6 Lacour-Gayet, iii, 273.
7 Rémusat, ii, 574.
8 Harris, 'Talleyrand and the British'.
9 Bernard, 538.
10 Greville, ed. Reeve, ii, 57.
11 Letter, 6 October 1830, Holland House Papers, British Library.
12 Ziegler, *Duchess of Dino*, 57.
13 Talleyrand, iii, 341.
14 Ibid., 342.
15 Ibid., 344.
16 Ibid., 454.
17 Lacour-Gayet, iii, 440.
18 Ibid., 247.
19 Talleyrand, iii, 343.

Chapter 3 · The Belgian Conference

1 Talleyrand, iii, 340.
2 Ibid., 353.
3 Daudet, 168.
4 Ibid.
5 Talleyrand, iii, 405.
6 Cooper, 341.
7 Ziegler, *Duchess of Dino*, 200.
8 Talleyrand, iii, 459.
9 Longford, 227.
10 Talleyrand, iii, 460.
11 Lacour-Gayet, iii, 260.
12 Ridley, 127.
13 Talleyrand, iii, 395.
14 Dino, i, 215.

Chapter 4 · Social Successes

1 Ziegler, *Duchess of Dino*, 197.
2 Stanhope, 4.
3 Greville, ed. Lloyd, 123.
4 Granville, ii, 68.
5 Ibid., 70.
6 Cooper, 350.
7 Greville, ed. Lloyd, 123.

8   Mitchell, 23; Liechtenstein, i, 158.
9   Macaulay, iii, 325 [from *Edinburgh Review*, July 1841].
10 Mitchell, 278.
11 Talleyrand, iii, 410.
12 Ibid., 411.
13 Bourgeois, 483.
14 Talleyrand, iii, 422.
15 Ibid., 425.
16 Ibid., 431.
17 Ridley, 129.

Chapter 5 · The Search for a Monarch

1   Bernard, 557.
2   Ibid.
3   Raikes, i, 89.
4   Talleyrand, iii, 467.
5   Ziegler, *Duchess of Dino*, 208.
6   Talleyrand, iii, 428.
7   Ibid., iv, 247.
8   Ibid., 106.
9   Ibid., 83.
10 Ibid., 112.
11 Ibid., 136.
12 Ibid.
13 Ibid., 137.

Chapter 6 · The Eighteen Articles

1   Lamartine, x, 390.
2   Balzac, 1,098.
3   Talleyrand, iv, 101.
4   Ibid., 117.
5   Ibid., 151.
6   Lacour-Gayet, iii, 274.
7   Bernard, 108.
8   Talleyrand, iv, 99.
9   Ibid., 236.
10 Ibid., 235.
11 Ibid., 239.
12 Holland, ed. Kriegel, 13.

Chapter 7 · French Troops in Belgium!

1   Lacour-Gayet, iii, 429.
2   Raikes, i, 74.
3   Lacour-Gayet, iii, 490.
4   Talleyrand, iii, 414.

5   Ibid., iv, 254.
6   Ridley, 135.
7   Talleyrand, iv, 288.
8   Ibid.
9   Greville, ed. Reeve, ii, 193.
10 Dino, i, 4.
11 Bernard, 539.
12 Talleyrand, iv, 397.
13 *The Times*, 30 September 1831.
14 Ibid.
15 Ibid.
16 Talleyrand, iv, 315.

Chapter 8 · 'A Firm and Cordial *Entente*'

1   Talleyrand, iv, 312.
2   Ibid., 344.
3   Webster, i, 111.
4   Talleyrand, iv, 344.
5   Webster, i, 91.
6   Daudet, 186.
7   Webster, i, 146.
8   Ibid.
9   Talleyrand, iv, 414.
10 Ilchester, 146.
11 Talleyrand, iv, 333.
12 Holland, ed. Kriegel, 115.
13 Ibid., 117.

Chapter 9 · The Triumph of Reform

1   Talleyrand, iv, 379.
2   Ibid., 382.
3   Ibid., 391.
4   Ibid., 395.
5   Webster, i, 97.
6   Raikes, i, 64.
7   Talleyrand, iv, 429.
8   Ibid., 423.
9   Holland, ed. Kriegel, 153.
10 Greville, ed. Reeve, ii, 270.
11 Lamartine, ii, 307.
12 Cooper, 332.
13 Dino, i, 41.
14 Talleyrand, iv, 448.
15 Ibid., 451.
16 Ibid., 456.

17 Lady Holland, 137.
18 Rémusat, ii, 576.

Chapter 10 · Leave of Absence

1   Talleyrand, iv, 479.
2   Bernardy, 199.
3   Ziegler, *Duchess of Dino*, 212.
4   Lacour-Gayet, iii, 267.
5   Bernardy, 198.
6   Price, 233.
7   Talleyrand, iv, 467.
8   Ibid., 469.
9   Ibid., 480.
10 Holland, ed. Kriegel, 193.
11 Lacour-Gayet, iii, 287.
12 Talleyrand, v, 4.
13 Ibid.
14 Lacour-Gayet, iii, 289.
15 Dino, i, 20.
16 Letter, September 1832, Holland House Papers, British Library.
17 Talleyrand, v, 5.
18 Ibid., 39.
19 Ibid., 22.
20 Holland, ed. Kriegel, 204.

Chapter 11 · Besieging Antwerp

1   Talleyrand, v, 53.
2   Webster, i, 173.
3   Ibid., 174.
4   Lacour-Gayet, iii, 293.
5   Thornbury, iv, 151.
6   Lacour-Gayet, iii, 441.
7   Waresquiel, 792.
8   Lacour-Gayet, iii, 259.
9   Webster, i, 109.
10 Talleyrand, v, 88.
11 Ibid., 114.
12 Ibid., iii, 402.
13 Creevey, 343.

Chapter 12 · A New Challenge

1   Holland, ed. Kriegel, 211.
2   Talleyrand, v, 145.
3   Holland, ed. Kriegel, 342.
4   Lacour-Gayet, iii, 203.

5   Talleyrand, v, 162.
6   Ibid., 171.
7   Ibid., 293.
8   Bernard, 575.
9   Mérimée, i, 91–2.
10 Dino, i, 268.
11 Ibid., 64.
12 Talleyrand, v, 269.
13 Dino, i, 31.
14 Talleyrand, v, 291.

Chapter 13 · The Quadruple Alliance

1   Lacour-Gayet, iii, 296.
2   Webster, i, 386.
3   Talleyrand, v, 327.
4   Daudet, 185.
5   Ibid., 186.
6   Talleyrand, v, 325.
7   Daudet, 183.
8   Talleyrand, v, 363.
9   Ibid., 383.
10 Webster, i, 396.
11 Talleyrand, v, 387.

Chapter 14 · A Changing Scene

1   Webster, i, 396.
2   Ibid., 398.
3   Dino, i, 128.
4   Ibid., 104.
5   Ibid., 230.
6   Ibid., 75.
7   Ibid., 48.
8   Ibid., 114.
9   Ibid., 115.
10 Ibid., 54.
11 Ibid., 86.
12 Ibid., 78.
13 Ibid., 114.
14 Ibid., 94.
15 Ibid., 141.
16 Talleyrand, v, 446.
17 Ibid., 448.
18 Ziegler, *Duchess of Dino*, 232.
19 Ibid., 220.
20 Ibid., 198.
21 Ibid., 214.

Chapter 15 · Time to Go

1   Letter, 23 September 1833, Holland House Papers, British Library.
2   Letter [Jan–March 1830], Holland House Papers, British Library.
3   Webster, i, 409.
4   Dino, i, 225.
5   Ibid., 231.
6   Lacour-Gayet, iii, 334.
7   Ibid., 322.
8   Dino, i, 262.
9   Lacour-Gayet, iii, 316.
10 Mirabeau, 207.
11 Ibid., 216.
12 Ibid., 225.
13 Ibid., 239.
14 Ibid., 243.
15 Ibid., 215.

Epilogue

1   Waresquiel, 784.
2   Dino, i, 301.
3   Cooper, 374.
4   Greville, ed. Lloyd, 123.

Bibliography

Books

Antonetti, Guy, *Louis-Philippe* (Paris, 1994)

Arbuthnot, Harriet, *The Journal of Mrs Arbuthnot, 1820–1832*, 2 vols (London, 1950)

Balzac, Honoré de, *Oeuvres complètes*, i: *Le Père Goriot* (Paris, 1911)

Barère, Bertrand, *Mémoires*, ii (Paris, 1842)

Bernard, J. F., *Talleyrand* (London, 1973)

Bernardy, Françoise de, *Son of Talleyrand: The Life of Comte Charles de Flahaut*, trans. Lucy Norton (London, 1956)

Bourgeois, Émile, 'Reaction and revolution in Paris' and 'The Orléans dynasty', in A. W. Wark, G. W. Prothero and S. Leathes (eds), *The Cambridge Modern History*, x: *The Restoration* (Cambridge, 1907)

Bourne, Kenneth, *Palmerston: The Early Years* (London, 1982)

Brisville, Jean-Claude, *Le souper* (Paris, 1989)

Burney, Fanny, *The Journals and Letters of Fanny Burney*, ed. Joyce Hemlow and Althea Douglas, ii (Oxford, 1972)

Calasso, Roberto, *The Ruin of Kasch*, trans. William Weaver and Stephen Sartarelli (Cambridge, MA, 1994)

Castelot, André, *Talleyrand ou le cynisme* (Paris, 1977)

Charmley, John, *The Princess and the Politicians* (London, 2005)

Cooper, Duff, *Talleyrand* (New York, 1997)

Creevey, Thomas, *Creevey*, ed. John Gore (London, 1949)

Daudet, Ernest, *Une vie d'ambassadrice au siècle dernier: la princesse de Lieven* (Paris, 1919)

Dino, Duchesse de, *Chronique de 1831 à 1862*, ed. Princesse Radziwill, 4 vols (Paris, 1909)

Doyle, John, *Political Sketches by H. B.*, i (1829–30), ii (1831–2)

Granville, Harriet, Countess, *Letters*, ed. F. Leveson-Gower, 2 vols (1894)

Greville, Charles, *The Greville Memoirs*, ed. Henry Reeve, 3 vols (London, 1874)

——— *The Greville Memoirs*, ed. Christopher Lloyd (London, 1947)

Harris, Robin, *Talleyrand: Betrayer and Saviour of France* (London, 2007)

Holland, Elizabeth, Lady, *Letters of Elizabeth, Lady Holland to Her Son*, ed. Lord Ilchester (London, 1946)

Holland, third Lord, *The Holland House Diaries, 1831–1840*, ed. Abraham D. Kriegel (London, 1977)

Hyde, H. Montgomery, *Princess Lieven* (London, 1938)

Ilchester, Earl of, *Chronicles of Holland House, 1820–1900* (London, 1937)

Kelly, Linda, *Women of the French Revolution* (London, 1986)

————*Juniper Hall: An English Refuge from the French Revolution* (London, 1991)

————*The Young Romantics: Writers and Liaisons, Paris 1827–37* (London, 2003)

————*Holland House: A History of London's Most Celebrated Salon* (London, 2013)

Lacour-Gayet, G., *Talleyrand 1754–1838*, 3 vols (Paris, 1932)

Lamartine, Alphonse de, *Cours familier de littérature*, 28 vols (1856–69)

Lawday, David, *Napoleon's Master: A Life of Prince Talleyrand* (London, 2007)

Liechtenstein, Princess, *Holland House*, 2 vols (1874)

Longford, Elizabeth, *Pillar of State* (London, 1972)

Macaulay, Thomas Babington, *Critical and Historical Essays*, iii (1854)

Madelin, Louis, *Talleyrand* (Paris, 1944)

Mérimée, Prosper, *Correspondance générale*, 2 vols (Paris, 1941–2)

Mirabeau, Comtesse de, *Le prince de Talleyrand et la maison d'Orléans* (Paris, 1890)

Mitchell, Leslie, *Holland House* (London, 1980)

Orieux, Jean, *Talleyrand ou le sphinx incompris* (Paris, 1970)

Paléologue, Maurice, *Romantisme et diplomatie: Talleyrand, Metternich, Chateaubriand* (Paris, 1928)

Pallain, G., *L'ambassade de Talleyrand à Londres* (Paris, 1878)

Price, Munro, *The Perilous Crown: France between Revolutions* (London, 2007)

Raikes, Thomas, *A Portion of the Journal Kept by Thomas Raikes, Esq., from 1831 to 1847*, i (1856)

Rémusat, Charles, Comte de, *Mémoires de ma vie*, 5 vols (Paris, 1858–67)

Ridley, Jasper, *Lord Palmerston* (London, 1970)

Sainte-Beuve, Charles-Augustin, *M. de Talleyrand* (Paris, 1870)

Stanhope, Earl, *Notes of Conversations with the Duke of Wellington 1831–1851*, with introduction by Elizabeth Longford (London, 1998)

Talleyrand, Prince de, *Mémoires*, ed. Duc de Broglie, 5 vols (Paris, 1892)

Thornbury, George Walter, *Old and New London*, 6 vols (1878)

Waresquiel, Emmanuel de, *Talleyrand: le prince immobile* (Paris, 2015)

Webster, Sir Charles, *The Foreign Policy of Palmerston*, i: *1830–1841* (London, 1951)

Ziegler, Philip, *The Duchess of Dino* (London, 1962)

————*William IV* (London, 1970)

Lectures

Harris, Robin, 'Talleyrand and the British'. Lecture delivered at the Travellers Club, London, 18 May 2007. Available at http://talleyrand.org/TalleyrandBe/talleyrand_and_the_british.html (accessed 20 September 2016)

Mansel, Philip, 'London, Paris, Brussels: the creation of Belgium'. Lecture delivered at the Belgian embassy, London, 1992

Catalogue

Hünersdorff, Richard von, *Charles-Maurice de Talleyrand-Périgord: A Collection of Books, Prints, Autographs, Drawings and Manuscripts Spanning a Life in Diplomacy* (London, 2012)

Manuscript sources

Letters from Talleyrand to Lord and Lady Holland, Holland House Papers, British Library [Add. MS 51635]

Index

Aberdeen, George Hamilton Gordon, 4th Earl of: discusses Belgium with Talleyrand, 20, 27; good relations with Talleyrand, 26; attends London Conference on Belgium, 33; attacks French occupation of Ancona, 86

Adélaïde, Madame (Louis-Philippe's sister): and accession of Louis-Philippe to throne, 13; correspondence with Talleyrand, 19, 24, 33, 52, 80, 120; and Talleyrand's appointment to London embassy, 19–20, 33; and Talleyrand's differences with Molé, 24–5; Duchess of Dino writes to, 26, 31; and Talleyrand's popularity in London, 31, 33; and Talleyrand's choice of monarch for Belgium, 47; Périer resents, 51; and Talleyrand's overwork, 57; and treaty settling Belgian independence, 77; in Talleyrand's memoirs, 82; sees Talleyrand as successor to Périer, 88; and Anglo-French convention on Netherlands, 98; friendship with Princesse de Vaudémont, 103; hopes for Talleyrand's return to London, 139; respect for Talleyrand, 143; and Talleyrand's resignation, 143–5; and Talleyrand's death, 151

Adelaide, Queen of William IV, 57, 111, 129

Alexander I, Tsar of Russia, 30

Alien Bill (Britain, 1793), 8

Ancona (Italy), 85–6

Antwerp: controlled by Dutch, 33, 49, 64; offered to Britain, 41; Talleyrand opposes English acquisition of, 66; Dutch evacuation, 76, 84, 92, 97–8, 100; Dutch king refuses to accept terms over, 101; siege and surrender to French force, 101–2, 110, 117

Austria: war with France, 1; suppresses risings in Italy, 49–50; intervenes in Papal States, 84–5; and ratification of Belgian independence, 84, 88, 97, 99; prevents domestic revolution, 107; persuades Dutch king to accept Belgian settlement, 111; signs Convention of Münchengrätz, 116; interferes in Switzerland, 117

Bacourt, Adolphe de: as Duchess de Dino's lover, 48–9, 57, 75, 118, 129, 138; as Talleyrand's first secretary in London, 48; collapse, 57; edits Talleyrand's memoirs, 82, 128; letter from Talleyrand convalescing at Rochecotte, 96; takes charge of London embassy in Talleyrand's absence, 115; and Talleyrand's return to London, 118

Balzac, Honoré de: Le Père Goriot, 55

Barante, Prosper de, 139

Barère, Bertrand, 1

Bases de séparation (on Belgium), 60, 75

Bedford, John Russell, 6th Duke of, 40

Belgium: revolts against Dutch rule (1830), 15–16, 20, 24–6, 28, 149; London Conference on (1830–1), 33–4, 41–3, 75–6, 97, 108; breaks from Austria (1790), 34; refuses Prince of Orange as king, 34, 41; granted independence, 43–4, 84; selection of monarch, 46; independence guaranteed, 49;

Belgium (*cont.*): Talleyrand's pessimism over survival, 50; Leopold elected king, 60; renewed crisis (1832), 60; Dutch army invades, 64–5, 67; French troops in, 64, 67, 71; demolition of fortresses, 67–8, 77–9, 83–4; signs Twenty-Four Articles (treaty), 76–7; Dutch resistance to indpendence, 97–8; and Anglo-French convention against Dutch, 98–9; French troops withdraw from after fall of Antwerp, 102; Dutch accept settlement over, 112

Benckendorff, Count Alexander (Princess Lieven's brother), 78

Berry, Maria Carolina, Duchesse de, 57, 93, 110

Blanc, Louis, 42

Bligh, Sir John Duncan, 132

Bonaparte, Jérôme, 130

Bonaparte, Joseph, 58

Bonaparte, Lucien, 58

Bordeaux, Henri, Duc de, 57

Bourbon-l'Archambault (spa), 96

Bowood, Wiltshire (house), 4

Bresson, Charles-Joseph, Comte, 21, 34, 48–9

Britain: French émigrés in, 4–7; outbreak of war with France (1793), 6–7; French émigrés expelled, 8; Talleyrand appointed ambassador to (1830), 9, 18; Talleyrand advocates French alliance with, 16–17, 66–7, 77, 117, 119; political changes, 19; social morality, 21; Talleyrand opposes presence on Continent, 66; discontent and demonstrations in, 80; ratifies Belgian independence, 84; cholera epidemic (1832), 87; unrest and near civil war, 89; insists on Belgian independence, 97; convention with France to use force aainst Dutch, 99–100; *see also* London; Reform Bill

Broglie, Victor François, 3rd Duc de: Talleyrand writes to from Bourbon-l'Archambault, 96; and French intervention in Belgium, 101; appointed foreign minister, 104; relations

with Talleyrand, 105–6, 116; grants Talleyrand extended leave of absence, 115; and proposed defensive alliance with Britain, 117, 119; deals direct with Palmerston, 120; resigns as foreign minister, 122

Bülow, Baron Heinrich von, 33

Burke, Edmund, 6

Burney, Fanny (Madame d'Arblay), 6–7

Byron, George Gordon, 6th Baron: *Don Juan*, 19

Calasso, Roberto: *The Ruin of Kasch*, 151–2

Canning, Sir Stratford, 121–2

Carlists, 110

Carlos, Don, 107, 123

Castlereagh, Robert Stewart, Viscount (*later* 2nd Marquess of Londonderry), 72, 83

Charles X, King of France, 9, 11–14, 29, 57, 110, 144

Charlotte, Princess (George IV's daughter), 47, 61

Chateaubriand, René, Vicomte de, 10

cholera epidemic (1832), 87

Cooper, Alfred Duff, 10

Cowper, Emily Mary, Countess (Amelia; *later* Viscountess Palmerston), 131

Creevey, Thomas, 30, 86, 108–9, 111

Crimean War (1854–6), 132

Dalberg, Emerich, Duc de, 82–3, 112

Danton, Georges Jacques: Talleyrand meets, 1–3

Daumier, Honoré, 147

Delacroix, Eugène: *Liberty Leading the People* (painting), 93–4

Dino, Dorothea, Duchesse de: on Talleyrand's reception at opening of British Parliament, 3; relations with Talleyrand, 11, 21, 133; and Talleyrand's appointment as ambassador, 15, 149; arrives in London, 21; success in society, 22–3, 30, 37–9, 86–7, 150; memoirs and journal, 23, 128–9; on Aberdeen's good opinion of Talleyrand, 26; relations with Princess Lieven, 30, 108–9, 132; dislikes Palmerston, 35–6, 132; on

Talleyrand's extravagance in London, 37; relations with Bacourt, 48, 57, 118, 129; and Princess Esterházy, 58; distrusts Montrond, 59; attends Queen Adelaide's drawing-room, 69; moves with Talleyrand to Hanover Square, 70; Comtesse de Flahaut disparages, 75; entertains Rémusat, 90–1; opposes Flahaut's appointment as Talleyrand's successor, 92; takes cure in Switzerland, 96; and Duc d'Orléans' visit to London, 111; Montrond tricks, 113–14; bad treatment by French press, 114; on Talleyrand's possible return to England, 115, 140–1; accompanies Talleyrand on final return to London (1833), 117; mediates between Bacourt and Talleyrand, 119; frustrated by rejection of Talleyrand's suggested treaty, 120; and Palmerston's brusqueness towards Talleyrand, 128; recounts time in London, 128–30; on Esterházy's leaving London, 131; on Palmerston at departure dinner for Lievens, 131; urges Talleyrand to retire, 133–5, 138; leaves England (1834), 138; entertains at Valençay, 140; George Sand describes, 142; drafts Talleyrand's letter of resignation, 143; political views, 150; on Talleyrand's popularity in Paris, 150
Dino, Pauline de (Dorothea's daughter), 11, 37
Doyle, John ('HB'), 78
Duncannon, John Ponsonby, Viscount, 133
Durham, John George Lambton, 1st Earl of, 121

Eighteen Articles (on Belgium), 60, 75–6, 106
Enghien, Louis de Bourbon-Condé, Duc de, 54
entente cordiale (France–Britain), 77
Esterházy, Prince Paul Antal, 33, 35, 108, 127, 131
Esterházy, Princess Maria Theresia, 57–8, 131

Falck, Anton-Reinhard, Baron, 33
Ferdinand VII, King of Spain, 106, 122
Flahaut de la Billarderie, Adélaïde, Comtesse de: moves to London, 5; as Talleyrand's mistress, 5; affair with Lansdowne's son, 6, 20; brings up Flahaut's illegitimate son, 58; *Adèle de Sénange* (novel), 7
Flahaut de la Billarderie, Alexandre-Sébastien, Comte de (Adélaïde's first husband), 5
Flahaut de la Billarderie, Auguste Charles Joseph, Comte de (Talleyrand's son): taken to London as child, 5; appointed special envoy to London, 41–2, 46; as father of Hortense's son, 58; appointed ambassador in Berlin, 74; Dalberg on, 83; passed over as successor to Talleyrand in London, 92–3, 95; and Duc d'Orléans' visit to London, 111; malice towards Duchesse de Dino, 139; friendship with Duc d'Orléans, 141
Flahaut de la Billarderie, Margaret, Comtesse de (Viscountess Keith): schemes to take over London embassy for husband, 75; intrigues, 93, 99–100; criticises choice of Medem as chargé d'affaires, 131; malice towards Duchesse de Dino, 139; on Duchesse of Dino's influence on Talleyrand, 150
Fox, Charles, 22, 80
Fox, Charles James: welcomes Talleyrand, 4, 7, 19
France: war with Austria and Prussia, 1, 3; Enlightenment, 3; war with Britain (1793), 6–7; Revolutionary Terror, 7; Talleyrand restores as power at Congress of Vienna, 10; 1830 revolution, 13; and Belgian claim to independence, 15–16, 20, 24–5; Talleyrand advocates alliance with Britain, 16–17, 66, 77, 117, 119; and creation of Netherlands, 28; ministerial crisis (1831), 31; and grant of independence to Belgium, 45–6, 61, 77, 84; revolutions (1831), 49; Périer forms government, 51; Second Republic, 54; troops in Belgium against Dutch invasion, 64, 67, 71;

France (*cont.*): insurrections and unrest, 79, 149–50; and demolition of Belgian fortresses, 83–4; intervention in Papal States, 85–6; June Rising (1832), 93–4; convention with Britain to use force for Belgian independence, 97–100; Soult forms government (1832), 97; besieges and takes Antwerp, 101; withdraws from Belgium after fall of Antwerp, 102; and Carlist hopes of succession, 110; and Palmerston's proposed joint treaty with Spain and Portugal, 123–5; *see also* Paris

French Revolution, 2–3, 113

Garrick, David, 6
Genlis, Stéphanie-Félicité Ducrest de St Aubin, Comtesse de, 5
George I, King of Great Britain, 24
Gérard, Marshal Maurice Étienne, Comte, 133
Germany: rising (1831), 49, 149
Goderich, Frederick John Robinson, Viscount, 72
Granville, Granville Leveson-Gower, 1st Earl, 40, 46, 68, 79, 105, 127, 137
Granville, Harriet, Countess (*née* Cavendish), 38–9
Greville, Charles, 18, 38–9, 69, 86, 151
Grey, Charles, 2nd Earl: influenced by Princess Lieven, 29, 108, 122; becomes prime minister (1831), 32; and French intervention in Belgium, 68; embarrassed by William IV's coronation speech, 69; rents Hanover Square house to Talleyrand, 70; Talleyrand's good relations with, 78, 86; and progress of Reform Bill, 80, 89; in Talleyrand's memoirs, 82; on French occupation of Ancona, 86; resigns and resumes premiership, 89; gives farewell dinner for Talleyrand, 95; and Palmerston's rudeness to Talleyrand, 105; rejects Talleyrand's suggested 'status quo' treaty, 119–20; as Duchess of Dino's confidant, 130; and departure of Princess Lieven, 131; retires (1834), 132, 134

Grey, Mary, Countess (*née* Ponsonby), 22, 30, 99

'HB' (cartoonist) *see* Doyle, John
Holland, Elizabeth, Lady: entertains at Holland House, 31, 39–40; anxiety over husband's losing office, 80; on death of Périer, 89; and Talleyrand's retirement, 137
Holland, Henry Richard Vassall Fox, 3rd Baron: friendship with Talleyrand, 20, 22, 30–1, 78–9; as chancellor of Duchy of Lancaster, 40; and Talleyrand's acceptance of M. le Hon., 62; and French intervention in Belgium, 68; defends Talleyrand against Londonderry's attack, 72; on fate of Belgian fortresses, 79; diaries, 81; on Duchesse de Berry's uprising, 93; and Talleyrand's departure from England, 95; buys Scheffer portrait of Talleyrand, 114; rejects Talleyrand's suggested 'status quo' treaty, 119
Holland House: salon, 30–1, 39–40, 78, 81, 95
Holy Alliance, 14, 16, 47, 116
Hortense (Bonaparte), Queen of Holland, 58
Hugo, Victor: on Talleyrand's appointment to London, 18; on June Rising, 93; *Les Misérables*, 93
Humboldt, Wilhelm von, 98, 108

Isabella, Dona (*later* Queen of Spain), 106
Italy: rising (1831), 49, 149

Jeffrey, Francis, 81
Jersey, Frances Villiers, Countess of, 38, 104
Johnson, Samuel, 6
Jordan, Dorothea, 22
Juniper Hall, Surrey, 6

Lamarque, General Jean-Maximilien, 93
Lamartine, Alphonse de, 37, 53–4; *Cours familier de littérature*, 53; *Les méditations poétiques*, 53
Lansdowne, Henry Petty-Fitzmaurice, 3rd Marquess of, 20

Lansdowne, William Petty, 1st Marquess of: welcomes Talleyrand, 4, 19; gives letters of introduction to Talleyrand for stay in America, 8

Latouche, Henri de, 113–14

Leopold I (of Saxe-Coburg), King of the Belgians: elected king, 47–8, 60–2; marriage to Louise, 48; and Dutch invasion of Belgium, 64, 68, 75; and terms of Belgian independence, 106

Leuchtenberg, Maximilien de Beauharnais, Duke of, 46–7

Lieven, Christopher, Prince, 33, 108, 127, 130–1

Lieven, Dorothea, Princess (née von Benckendorff): disapproves of Talleyrand's appointment to London, 29; influence on Grey, 29, 108, 122; relations with Duchess of Dino, 30, 108, 132; relations with Talleyrand, 30; discusses Belgium with Talleyrand, 65–6; at Queen Adelaide's drawing room, 69–70; on Talleyrand's status in London, 78; on Palmerston's differences with Cabinet over alliance with France, 99; Talleyrand on, 108; on Broglie's bypassing Talleyrand, 120; and dispute over Canning's appointment to Russia, 121–2; on Talleyrand's gambling, 121; leaves London, 131–2; and Dorothea's leaving London with Talleyrand, 138; respected in London, 150

London: Talleyrand's early 1792 mission to, 2, 4; French émigrés in, 4; Talleyrand on character, 19; Conference on Belgium, 33–4, 41–3, 75–6, 97, 108; cholera, 87; see also Britain

Londonderry, Charles William Stewart, 3rd Marquess of, 71–2, 78

Longwy (fortress), 1

Louis, Dominique, Baron, 88

Louis XVI, King of France: under threat, 2; Talleyrand's letters to, 5; executed, 6

Louis XVIII, King of France: accession, 10, 30; reign and policies, 11–12; death, 11

Louis-Philippe, King of France (earlier Duc d'Orléans): accession, 9, 13–15, 20, 30; 152; Talleyrand's good relations with and regard for, 12, 143; appoints Talleyrand ambassador to Britain, 15; Anglophilia, 16; advised by Mme Adélaïde, 20; and Molé's differences with Talleyrand, 24–5; and Belgian independence, 25–6, 45; popularity in London, 32; supports Talleyrand over Belgium, 42; and appointment of Belgian monarch, 46, 49; happy marriage, 48; and Périer government, 50–1; rule, 50–1; abdicates (1848), 54; and Princess Esterházy, 58; assassination attempts on, 79–80, 143; and destruction of Belgian fortresses, 79; Dalberg on first ministry, 83; avoids war with Austria over Papal States, 85; suppresses June Rising, 94; and Anglo-French convention against Dutch, 98; Princesse de Vaudémont's relations with, 103; takes over as foreign minister after Périer's death, 105; security, 127; French aristocracy's scornful view of, 138; hopes for Talleyrand's return to London, 139; ridiculed and caricatured, 142; receives Talleyrand's letters of resignation, 144–6; works for peace in Europe, 149–50; visits Talleyrand on deathbed, 151

Louise d'Orléans, Queen of Leopold I of Belgium, 48, 67

Luxembourg: and Belgian independence, 44, 60; Dutch recover eastern part, 76

Lyons: insurrection by silk workers, 79; unrest, 120

Maastricht: Belgians seize, 49

Macaulay, Thomas Babington, Baron, 40, 56

Mahmud II, Ottoman Emperor, 107

Mareuil, Baron Durand de, 92, 96, 99, 104

Maria II, Queen of Portugal, 106, 123

Marie Antoinette, Queen of Louis XVI: executed, 7

Marie-Amélie, Queen of Louis-Philippe, 48, 111

Marienberg (fortress), 83

Marseilles: unrest, 120

Matusiewicz, Auguste-Joseph, Count, 33, 76, 111

Medem, Count Paul Ivanovich, 131–2

Mehemet Ali, Viceroy of Egypt, 107

Melbourne, William Lamb, 2nd Viscount, 81, 133, 139, 145

Mérimée, Prosper, 103, 113

Metternich, Prince Clemens Lothar Wenzel von, 98

Miguel, Dom (*later* King of Portugal), 106, 123

Mirabeau, Honoré Gabriel Riqueti, Comte de, 54

Molé, Louis-Mathieu, Comte: as foreign minister, 20; hostility to Talleyrand, 24–5; intervenes in Belgian dispute, 24, 28; resigns, 31; communicates with Wellington, 104

Montrond, Casimir, Comte de, 58–9, 92, 97, 103, 113

Morny, Charles, 1st Duc de, 58

Münchengrätz, Convention of (1833), 116–17, 125

Musset, Alfred de, 141

Napoleon I (Bonaparte), Emperor of the French: Talleyrand disavows, 10; on British as nation of shopkeepers, 19; Talleyrand serves, 23; disparages Talleyrand, 25; Talleyrand's remark on death of, 38; and execution of Duc d'Enghien, 54; family in London, 58

Napoleon III, Emperor of the French (*earlier* Louis-Napoléon), 58

Narbonne, Louis-Marie, Comte de, 6, 8

National (newspaper), 12

Nemours, Louis Charles d'Orléans, Duc de, 46–7

Nesselrode, Charles Robert, Count, 65, 98

Netherlands: and Belgian claim to independence, 15–16, 27–8, 33; controls Antwerp, 33, 49; and London Conference on Belgium, 33–4, 41; and grant of Belgian independence, 43–4, 60, 75–7, 84, 91, 97, 106; agrees to Leopold as Belgian king, 48; army invades Belgium, 64–5, 67; reluctance to evacuate Antwerp, 97–8; Anglo-French joint action against, 98–100; accepts Belgian settlement, 112, 115

Nicholas I, Tsar of Russia, 121–2, 127, 130

Ord, Elizabeth, 108

Orléans, Ferdinand-Philippe, Duc d', 110–11, 139–41, 143, 145

Ottoman Empire (Turkey), 107, 121

Ouvrard, Gabriel, 25, 102

Palmerston, Henry John Temple, 3rd Viscount: succeeds Aberdeen as foreign secretary, 34; on Belgian settlement, 35, 44; relations with Talleyrand, 35–6, 78, 104–5, 121–2, 127–8; and Holland's indiscretions, 40; private letters to Granville in Paris, 40, 46, 68; proposes Leopold as Belgian king, 47; supports Reform Bill, 56; on Montrond's attendance on Talleyrand, 59; loses seat and re-elected (1831), 60; advocates British alliance with France, 67; on Dutch invasion of Belgium, 67; and destruction of Belgian fortresses, 68, 83; persuades Van de Weyer to agree to Twenty-Four Articles on Belgium, 76; on *entente* with France over Belgian independence, 77; caricatured by 'HB', 78; in Talleyrand's memoirs, 82; denies non-intervention, 84; intercedes in French dispute over Papal States, 85; and Talleyrand's taking leave, 91; good wishes to Talleyrand on departure, 95; Princess Lieven gossips about, 99; on King of Holland's intrigue with Ouvrard, 102; and Ottoman conflict with Mehemet Ali, 107; and Talleyrand's proposed return to London, 115; coolness over Talleyrand's suggested 'status quo' treaty, 119–20; anger at Russian refusal to accept Canning as ambassador, 121–2; proposes treaty with Spain and Portugal (Quadruple Alliance), 123–7; and Talleyrand's revealing Quadruple Alliance to northern powers, 127–8; and Lievens' departure, 131; disliked by Princess Lieven and Duchess of Dino, 132; gives farewell dinner for Talleyrand, 135; on Talleyrand's political partialities in England, 137; and Talleyrand's resignation, 145

Paris: prisoners massacred (September 1792), 2–3; in 1830 revolution, 13; riots in support of Belgian revolutionaries, 28; demonstrations against Russian occupation of Warsaw, 70; cholera, 87–8; in June Rising (1832), 93–4; *see also* France

Pedro, Dom (*sometime* King of Portugal and Emperor of Brazil), 106, 123

Périer, Casimir: premiership, 51–2, 55, 79; Talleyrand's good relations with, 84; sends troops to Ancona (Italy), 85–6; death from cholera, 88–9

Petre, Laura Maria, 38, 135

Philippeville (fortress), 83

Phillips, Susanna, 6

Piscatory, Émile, 114

Place, Francis, 89

Poland: revolt against Russian rule, 42, 49–50, 70, 107, 149

Polignac, Jules, Prince de: appointed chief minister by Charles X, 12; rioters demand death penalty for, 28; Princess Lieven criticises, 29; trial and sentence, 31, 42–3

Ponsonby, John, Viscount, 23

Portugal: civil war, 106; civil war ends, 122; Palmerston proposes joint treaty with (Quadruple Alliance), 123–5

Prussia: war with France, 1; acquires former French territories of Rhine, 25; suppresses rising in Germany, 49–50; neutrality in Russia-Poland dispute, 74; and ratification of Belgian independence, 84, 88, 97, 99; prevents domestic revolution, 107; persuades Dutch king to accept Belgian settlement, 111; signs Convention of Münchengrätz, 116

Quadruple Alliance (Britain-France-Portugal-Spain), 124–8, 133

Railes, Thomas, 63

Reform Bill (Britain, 1831–2), 50, 55–6, 59, 80, 86–8, 91, 140, 150

Reichstadt, François Charles Joseph Bonaparte, Duc de ('Napoleon II'): death, 94

Rémusat, Charles, Comte de, 21, 89–90

revolutions of 1848, 53–4

Rigny, Henri, Comte de, 122, 125–6, 133

Robespierre, Maximilien, 9

Rochecotte (chateau), Touraine, 96

Russell, Lord William, 40

Russia: Poland revolts against (1831), 42, 49–50, 107; occupies Warsaw, 70, 74; and ratification of Belgian independence, 84, 88, 97, 99; treaty with Turkey (1833), 107; persuades Dutch king to accept Belgian settlement, 111; signs Convention of Münchengrätz, 116; encroachment in Turkey, 117, 121; refuses to accept Canning as ambassador, 121; and Dardanelles, 132

Sainte-Beuve, Charles-Augustin, 82

Sand, George, 141

Scheffer, Ary: portrait of Talleyrand, 114

Sébastiani, François Horace Bastien, Comte: as foreign minister, 41, 105; and Belgian question, 41–2, 45, 61; and Russian threat to Poland, 49; and disorder in Europe, 50; Talleyrand's good relations with, 51–2; Talleyrand writes to on Reform Bill debates, 56; and Talleyrand's advocacy of alliance with Britain, 66; favours destruction of Belgian fortresses, 68; Dalberg on effects of stroke, 83; ill health, 88; favours Flahaut as Talleyrand's successor in London, 96; appointed ambassador to London on Talleyrand's resignation, 147

Sheridan, Richard Brinsley, 6

Smith, Sydney, 81

Soult, Marshal Nicolas Jean-de-Dieu: forms government, 97–8; resigns, 133

Spain: civil war ends, 122; Palmerston proposes joint treaty with (Quadruple Alliance), 123–5; violence in, 133

Staël, Anne-Louise-Germaine Necker, Baronne de: in England, 6–7; returns to Switzerland, 8; Talleyrand discards, 9; *Corinne*, 87

Stendhal (Marie-Henri Beyle), 113

Swiss Guard: massacred in Tuileries, 2

Switzerland: Austria attempts to alter
  constitution, 117

Talleyrand, Catherine de (*née* Grand;
  Princesse de Bénévent): marriage to
  Talleyrand, 11
Talleyrand-Périgord, Charles-Maurice
  de: meets Danton, 1–3; attitude to
  French Revolution, 2–4; mission
  to London (early summer 1792), 2,
  4–5; excommunicated, 4; lameness,
  4; accused of treachery, property
  confiscated and proscribed, 5; leaves
  England (1794) and sails for America,
  7; appointed ambassador to London
  (1830), 9, 14–15, 18–19; career after
  expulsion, 9–10; financial dealings, 10,
  25; marriage to Catherine Grand, 11;
  relations with Duchesse de Dino, 11,
  21, 133; regard for Louis-Philippe, 12,
  143; and accession of Louis-Philippe, 14;
  advocates French alliance with Britain,
  16–17, 66–7, 77, 117, 119–20; friendship
  with Lord Holland, 20, 22, 30–1, 78–9;
  appearance, 21, 103; staff in London, 21;
  audience with and address to William IV,
  23–4, 27; Molé's hostility to, 24–5; and
  Belgian claims to independence, 25–6,
  28–9; Princess Lieven criticises, 29; at
  London Conference on Belgium, 32–4,
  41, 43–4; relations with Palmerston, 35,
  36, 78, 127–8; pet dog, 37; social life
  in London, 37–40, 103; conversation
  and wit, 38–40, 81, 86; popularity in
  London, 38–9, 45, 114; loses claims to
  Luxembourg and frontier districts, 44;
  and grant of independence to Belgium,
  45–6; abused in France for Belgian
  settlement, 46; and choice of monarch
  for Belgium, 46–7; attempts mediation
  in Poland, 49; attitude to Dorothea's
  younger lovers, 49; pessimism over
  Belgian survival, 50; welcomes Périer
  as prime minister, 51–2; confides in
  Lamartine, 53–4; Balzac praises, 55; and
  British Reform Bill, 56–7, 59; overwork
  and health problems, 57, 60; relations

with Montrond, 58–9; and renewed
  Belgian crisis (1832), 60–2; dressing and
  daily routine, 63; and Dutch invasion
  of Belgium, 64, 67; discusses partition
  of Belgium with Princess Lieven, 65–6;
  attends William IV's coronation, 69;
  moves to Hanover Square, 70; attacked
  by Londonderry over French presence
  in Belgium, 71–2; caricatured by 'HB',
  78; good relations with Grey, 78, 86; on
  demolition of Belgian fortresses, 79,
  83–4; anxiety over assassination attempt
  on French royal family, 80; memoirs,
  81–2, 85, 128; on non-intervention, 84;
  anger at Périer's sending troops to Italy,
  85–6; declines premiership in succession
  to Périer, 88–90; ageing, 90–1; takes
  leave of absence, 91, 115; appalled by
  June rising in France, 94; final weeks
  in London, 95; returns to England,
  97; and Anglo-French convention for
  action against Dutch, 98–9, 101; alleged
  speculations with Ouvrard, 102; and
  death of Princesse de Vaudémont, 102–
  3; gambling, 103, 121; rinses nose, 104;
  on business of House of Commons, 106;
  and Middle East problem, 107; portrays
  diplomatic colleagues, 108; aversion
  to Flahaut, 111; and Duc d'Orléans'
  visit to London, 111; and Dutch king's
  acceptance of Belgian settlement, 112;
  on effect of French Revolution, 113;
  abused in French opposition press, 114;
  Scheffer portrait, 114; returns to France,
  (1831), 96; (1833), 115; urged to return
  to London, 115; final return to London
  (1833), 117; proposed 'status quo'
  treaty rejected, 119–20; and Broglie's
  resignation, 122; and Palmerston's
  proposed treaty with Spain and Portugal
  (Quadruple Alliance), 123–7; signs
  Quadruple Alliance, 128; and Esterházy's
  departure, 131; leaves London (1834)
  and hesitates over retirement, 133–8,
  140, 143; on Melbourne's government,
  133; disparaged by George Sand, 141–2;
  and death of Princess Tyszkiewicz, 143;

sends letters of resignation, 143, 145–6; discusses political situation in England and France with Louis-Philippe, 147; achievements and tributes, 149–52; praised in France, 150; death, 151

Tellier, M. (Talleyrand's secretary), 57

Thiers, Adolphe: founds *National* (newspaper), 12; in 1830 revolution, 13; as minister of interior under Soult, 97; admitted to Académie française, 150

Tory party: repressive government, 4; rule under Wellington, 19; opposes Reform Bill, 88, 89; returns to power (1834), 145

Travellers Club, London, 64, 103, 121

Turkey *see* Ottoman Empire

Twenty-Four Articles (on Belgium), 76, 98

Tyszkiewitz, Maria Theresa, Princess, 143, 145

Unkkar Sekelessi, treaty of (1833), 107

Valençay (chateau), 10–11, 139–41

Valmy, Battle of (1792), 3

Vaudémont, Louise, Princesse de (*née* Montmorency): Talleyrand's correspondence with, 20, 50, 52, 70, 73, 75, 81–5, 89, 91, 94, 99; death, 102; stays on in London, 115

Verdun, 1–2

Victoria, Princess (*later* Queen), 129

Vienna, Congress of (1815), 10, 15, 72, 149

Vincennes: fortress stormed, 331

Walpole, Horace: disparages Talleyrand, 4

Waresquiel, Emmanuel, 150

Warsaw: falls to Russians, 70, 74

Warwick Castle, 87

Webster, Sir Charles: *The Foreign Policy of Palmerston*, 102

Wellesley, Lord Charles, 9

Wellington, Arthur Wellesley, 1st Duke of: on Charles X, 12; as Prime Minister, 14, 19; good relations with Talleyrand, 15, 19, 26, 29; on accession of Louis-Philippe, 20; on Duchess of Dino's status, 22; Molé writes to on Belgian question, 24; and Belgian claim to independence, 28–9;

resigns premiership (1831), 32; defends Talleyrand against Londonderry's attack, 72–3; house attacked by rioters, 80; as prospective prime minister, 89, 120; on reformed House of Commons, 106; as Duchess of Dino's confidant, 130; returns to power on Melbourne's fall, 145; Talleyrand admires, 146

Wessenberg, Baron Johann Philippe von, 33, 108

Weyer, Sylvain Van de, 33, 50, 76

Whigs: welcome Talleyrand, 4; as opposition party, 19; Talleyrand renews contacts with, 19–20; form government under Grey (1831), 32–3, 59; and Reform Bill, 60, 86; and French revolutionary sympathies, 86; in reformed House of Commons, 106

William I, King of the Netherlands: and dominance over Belgium, 16, 26–8; and Belgian independence, 43; resents concessions to Belgium, 64, 101; William IV criticises for obstinacy, 77; refuses to withdraw troops from Antwerp, 97; reluctance to accept terms over Antwerp, 101, 105–6; deal with Ouvrard over grain supply, 102; agrees to settlement over Belgium, 111; danger of war with, 149

William IV, King of Great Britain: scorns Louis-Philippe, 22; Talleyrand meets and addresses, 22–4, 27; ancestry, 24; coronation, 69; criticises king of Netherlands, 77; invites Wellington to form government, 89; and Talleyrand's taking leave, 91; hostility to France, 99–100; promotes peaceful settlement with France, 119; and Adelaide's absence in Germany, 129; refuses to see Jérôme Bonaparte, 130; dislikes Melbourne, 133

William, Prince of Orange, 34, 41

Wycombe, John Henry Petty, Earl of (*later* 2nd Marquess of Lansdowne): affair with Mme de Flahaut, 6